The Volunteer Firefighters' Management Book

The Volunteer Firefighters' Management Book

Rob Stewart

The Bobbs-Merrill Company, Inc.
Indianapolis   New York

Copyright © 1982 by Rob Stewart

All rights reserved, including the right of reproduction in whole or in part in any form
Published by The Bobbs-Merrill Company, Inc.
Indianapolis   New York

Library of Congress Cataloging in Publication Data

Stewart, Rob.
    Volunteer firefighters' management book.
    1. Fire-departments—Management. I. Title.
TH9145.S787   363.3'78'068   81–18183
ISBN 0–672–52719–7   AACR2

Designed by Mary A. Brown
Manufactured in the United States of America

First printing

TO Nathaniel Stewart, *my father and the first author in my family,*

TO William C. Peck, *who has always demonstrated to me the finest qualities of the volunteer fire service,*

AND TO Peg Maloy, *who constantly encouraged me to strive to be a good writer.*

Contents

PREFACE 9

1. LEADERSHIP STYLES 11
2. PLANNING 32
3. PUBLIC RELATIONS 48
4. BUDGETING AND FINANCIAL MANAGEMENT 76
5. FIREGROUND OFFICER SELECTION 97
6. MORALE AND MOTIVATION: MANAGING THE VOLUNTEER 115
7. RECRUITMENT 131
8. LEGAL LIABILITIES 152
9. THE TRAINING FUNCTION 168
10. SELECTING AND PURCHASING FIRE APPARATUS 189

INDEX 219

Preface

In the spring of 1979 I started looking for books on fire department management. Several books had been published, and some of them were quite popular. Yet I verified my original concern: There was no book available that told a *volunteer fire officer,* at either the chief or the company level, how to manage effectively. That is why I wrote this book.

Some estimates say that there are slightly over 1 million volunteer firefighters in the United States. Others place the figure higher, at 2 million. Even the more conservative figure still means that the largest group of firefighters in this country are volunteers. They work at full-time jobs, five days or more a week, and still find time to protect and serve their communities. They give countless hours to training. They get out of bed in the middle of the night to answer fire alarms. All for no pay.

If you were to look at the historical progression of the volunteer spirit in America, you would find that the volunteer firefighter has his roots all the way back in prerevolutionary times. More important, he is one of the few remaining examples of the American volunteer spirit.

A volunteer fire officer who is keeping that tradition and spirit has some special needs. Like his paid counterpart, the volunteer officer has to manage and lead a force of professional firefighters. But that's where the similarity ends. The volunteer officer has to motivate his firefighters to stay active in the department and not quit. He has to budget financial resources that often get collected in unorthodox ways. He has to plan for fire prevention and protection in his community five or maybe ten years in the future. He has to recruit competent, mature, and interested community residents to join and serve, asking them to give up many hours of their free time. And he has to educate the public on what he and his volunteers do, sometimes fighting the misconception that they are paid to be firefighters. With many of these responsibilities, the volunteer fire officer may be performing skills that he does not normally practice at his regular job. That makes his job as a fire chief even tougher.

This book is for a chief. It's also for his officers, for they are the chiefs of tomorrow. It presents and discusses information about managing a volunteer fire department that the chief and his officers can relate to. It's about their special needs and their special responsibilities. It is not one of those general books on fire department management where only one fourth of the information is of any use to a volunteer fire officer.

I wrote *The Volunteer Firefighters' Management Book* so that the reader could understand it. It isn't steeped in extraterrestrial management philosophy plus difficult wording. Instead, it presents specific information about volunteer fire department management skills in a clear, easy-to-read way. And it backs up that information with examples of how to use it in the setting of a volunteer fire department. Each chapter in this book is important. The way the chapters are arranged is not a priority order. It is only a continuing list of management topics, and each is as valuable as the last one.

There is a special feeling about being a firefighter, and only a firefighter knows it. There's something even more special about being a *volunteer* firefighter. And only a volunteer knows that feeling. We have had that feeling and spirit for over two hundred years. We hope to keep it for another two hundred. That is why writing this book was a labor of love for me.

The Volunteer Firefighters' Management Book

The ultimate responsibility of any fire officer is to be an effective leader. Not everyone can direct the skills, abilities, and desires of many different individuals successfully. But that must not stop us from wanting to learn what good leadership is all about. It is a human quality the fire service has valued for over two hundred years, and certainly will for many more years to come.
—WILLIAM GOLDFEDER, LIEUTENANT,
MANHASSET-LAKEVILLE
FIRE DEPARTMENT NO. 3,
GREAT NECK, NEW YORK

1 / *Leadership Styles*

If you were to ask me what makes a man a good leader, I would say that a good leader is someone who acts and responds intelligently during crises. Many times we don't know who does or doesn't have leadership potential until a crisis occurs. It's no wonder, then, that people have traditionally held fire chiefs in high esteem. The chief commands his firefighters' actions in times of great danger and in emergency situations that can mean the difference between life and death. Without question, the fireground leader must have poise and self-control, and he must be able to make quick, precise decisions amid chaos and confusion.

A good fireground officer isn't a good leader only at the fire scene. He demonstrates good leadership skills all the time. For the fire officer, the quality of his leadership skills, or lack of them, as he manages his firefighters will directly affect how well those firefighters will respond to commands at the fire scene. A good leader thinks of his responsibilities and actions all the time; he works to maintain good relationships, as well as to change those factors that are hurting relationships with his personnel.

Leadership styles differ. What works for one officer may not work for another. Sometimes, leadership problems occur and there is no apparent, simple solution. Every leader must go through some self-assessment, especially during rough times. The question is, How do you go about it? Are there any scientific instruments designed to evaluate and measure management/leadership ability or identify strong and weak leadership areas? Is it better to be more "people oriented" than "goal oriented," or is an even blend of the two orientations best?

This chapter discusses two successful management/leadership models that the volunteer fire officer can use as easily as a corporate executive or production line manager can. They are good models for self-examination as you build on improving your leadership skills.

The Managerial Grid®

Robert R. Blake and Jane S. Mouton wrote *The Managerial Grid* in 1964.[1] Since that time, no other leadership style model has received so much attention and been used in more places in the world.

The Grid is an easy model to understand. There are two concerns depicted—a concern for production and a concern for people—and each has a measurement range from 1 to 9. A plotting of 1 (one) is the lowest level in the spectrum, and a plotting of 9 (nine) the highest.

In Figure 1.1, the horizontal axis represents a leader's concerns for *outcomes*.[2] Others define this axis in terms of *production* or *goals*. The vertical motivation scale represents the leader's concerns for people.

For instance, a manager who is very concerned about whether the members of his staff like him, at the expense of seeing to it that they do their work, is considered a 1,9-oriented manager or leader. He is extremely people and personality oriented, so much so that he will not pressure staff members to work because he thinks they won't approve of him if he requires them to work harder than they are currently doing.

The opposite of the 1,9-oriented manager is the 9,1-oriented manager, the manager who is totally immersed in the job. If he happens to be a plant production manager, then his

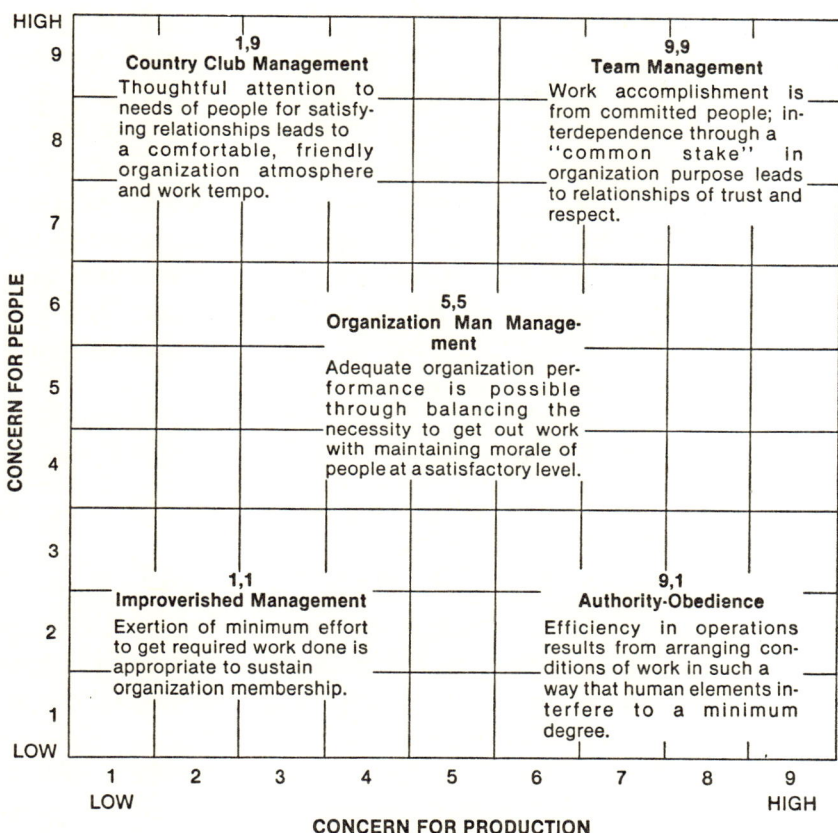

Figure 1.1 The Managerial Grid. From *The New Managerial Grid*, by Robert R. Blake and Jane Srygley Mouton. Houston: Gulf Publishing Company, Copyright © 1978, page 11. Reproduced by permission.

priority is production—and production alone. It makes no difference to him that some of the production manufacturing equipment may present a safety hazard, may need repair or a worker may be injured. And he isn't bothered that plant workers are being asked to meet production quotas in absolutely unrealistic time frames. Obviously, his 1 rating shows that he doesn't care about people, while the 9 score represents his determination to meet his production goals at any cost.

Other typical examples are the 1,1-oriented manager (poor with both people and outcomes) and the 5,5-oriented manager (no better than average).³ Those rankings reflect particular traits and behavior. Of course, what every leader or manager should try to achieve is a 9,9 ranking. This score reflects a leader who reaches all his goals and at the same time gets the best effort from his entire staff. He is concerned about people. *And* his people respect him and are eager to put forth their best effort in helping him achieve his goals. A caveat here: Keep in mind that a 9,9 ranking is a level of leadership that we work toward but don't always reach.

Where do you fit into all of this? How does the Grid help you as a fire chief? Let's go over some examples of how it does.

THE 9,1-ORIENTED FIRE OFFICER

The 9,1-oriented fire officer demonstrates his leadership style best at the fire scene. This is a situation that has a potentially great effect on both people and outcomes. The following story may get my point across:

David Grey is just completing his first six months as volunteer fire chief. A quiet, rather shy man, Grey has never been very close to any of the other volunteers. Nevertheless, through the years members have respected his skill on the fireground. So, a few years ago, he was a likely choice for lieutenant. Since that time he has slowly but steadily climbed up the ladder to the rank of chief of department. Yes, there were a few occasions when some members thought he ordered firefighters to take some unnecessary risks, but they never amounted to anything serious.

Whenever possible, a volunteer fire chief responds to all fires in town, and he is usually one of the first on the scene after the call goes in. This is true in our sample case. Chief Grey has arrived during the early evening hours at a working fire in a fire-resistant two-story brick commercial structure. He has learned that there is no civilian life hazard existing in the building. Yet, to control and extinguish the fire, he has ordered men to open up the roof. Other men are holding charged hand lines and are ready to begin an interior attack from the street.

His officers are baffled. They ask Chief Grey his reason for sending firefighters on the roof, as well as inside; both groups could be injured or killed if the roof or floor collapsed. The firefighters question Chief Grey because they know that there is no civilian life hazard at stake inside the building, and that the whole interior is on fire. But Chief Grey tells them to stop asking questions and carry out their orders.

Grey's regard for his firefighters' safety ranks around 1 on the concern-for-people scale, while his determination to put out the fire at any cost approaches 9 on the concern-for-outcome scale.

THE 1,9-ORIENTED FIRE OFFICER

What about the 1,9-oriented fire officer? How might he behave? I'll use Chief Davis as my example here, and you'll notice very different actions and decisions.

Chief Davis is speaking to his personnel at the monthly fire department business meeting. He is explaining that one of the first-due engines needs immediate repair or it may sustain extensive mechanical damage. This piece of apparatus is essential, for it responds to an area of high fire incidence. While Chief Davis is explaining all this, some members object to leaving the engine in the station on Saturday for repairs. They say it's a necessary piece of equipment to be on display in the upcoming parade, which also takes place on Saturday.

Chief Davis is a man who is always concerned about his firefighters' feelings toward him. He wants to remain popular with everyone, and so he gives in to their request to have the engine at the parade. He wants to please the men, and this fact becomes more important than getting the engine fixed and fully operational for fire responses.

Chiefs Grey and Davis are both hypothetical examples. They do, however, show us how we can use the Grid to look at a leader's behavior.

The 1,1 style is unrealistic and rare for a fire officer who is both administrator and fireground commander. Any volunteer officer who has little regard for his firefighters or who doesn't take the initiative to reach his goal, putting out the fire, probably won't become a chief. Nonetheless, understand that there are 1,1 leaders.

The 5,5–Oriented Fire Officer

The volunteer fire service probably has many officers who lead with a 5,5 Grid style. The 5,5–oriented leader is not a bad or incompetent officer. His strengths are that his firefighters respect him as a decision maker and administrator, on the fireground and off. His drawbacks are that he is content with the status quo, ordinary, and possibly mediocre. Why? He doesn't go beyond his present limits. He doesn't set enough personal challenges. He's satisfied to keep things on an even keel and not rock the boat.

How does the 5,5–oriented officer behave? He may, for instance, be having a problem getting local officials to cooperate with him and understand his needs. Instead of confronting the problem, he prefers to "test the wind" to find out how the majority thinks. That way he is not threatened by a loss of popularity with other members in the group. As for his actions on the fireground, this leader knows enough to do the job and control the fire. But he is not one to take advantage of training opportunities to improve his knowledge as a fireground commander. He knows what he needs to know, and that's enough.

The 9,9–Oriented Fire Officer

A leader who has a lot of concern for both people and outcomes is aiming for 9,9. Earlier, I said that the 9,9 leadership style is one we should aspire to, but not necessarily expect to reach. Because people interpret the Grid in their own way, one person may see a 9,9 orientation as unattainable, while another may believe he has seen leaders who already show all the 9,9

Leadership Styles

characteristics. I think that the exemplary traits of the 9,9 leadership style *are* achievable. There *are* managers and leaders who can inspire the greatest effort from their people and gain their desired outcomes, or even surpass their original goals.

What does this mean for the volunteer fire officer? What actions, mannerisms, decisions, and attitudes characterize the ultimate in leadership skill and ability.

- The 9,9–oriented volunteer officer knows what his firefighters are capable of. In administrative duties, when he delegates responsibility to subordinates, he selects people who are likely to succeed at their task. As a result, they get gratification from succeeding at a job, and the job also gets accomplished.
- The 9,9–oriented volunteer officer takes advantage of every opportunity to compliment firefighters whose actions are a credit to the department. He knows that morale and motivation are not human resource concerns to be taken lightly.
- The 9,9–oriented volunteer officer practices sound short- and long-range planning both in administrative and operational areas. He makes all his officers active participants in this process, which ultimately makes for a more professional, efficient, and functional fire department.
- The 9,9–oriented volunteer officer knows it's important to keep up with new and changing fire-suppression tactics and strategies. As a result, he makes future decisions as a fireground commander from a selection of approved alternatives that justify his actions and orders. In the end, the community benefits by a higher level of professional competence in their fire officer. So do his firefighters, whose safety and welfare depend on what they are told to do or not do at the fire scene.
- The 9,9–oriented volunteer officer asks for suggestions and ideas from his subordinates. Though there can be only one final decision maker in the organizational structure, his decisions don't preclude the advice and beliefs of others that can enhance department effectiveness. This is not to say that, at the fire scene, the officer expects his firefighters to come over and suggest how to fight the blaze. But it does mean that the officer listens to ideas for new, innovative operating procedures and fireground evolutions that will improve a firefighter's job. He knows that to cultivate talent and

potential leaders and officers for the future, he must first encourage them to think and suggest.
- The 9,9-oriented volunteer officer thinks about how outside groups affect the fire department. He asks, What outside agencies can help the fire department? Are we, the department, using these groups to their advantage? What outside groups hinder the fire department? What are the problems and how can they be remedied?

I hope that in reading over this list you discovered things you already do as an officer, things that show concern for both people and outcomes. The 9,9-oriented individual remains a standard of excellence that we should constantly strive to reach.

Updating the Grid

In 1978 Blake and Mouton improved on their thesis and wrote *The New Managerial Grid*.[4] They added more dimensions to their original hypothesis and responded to all the changes that had taken place, both in society and in managerial styles, since their original idea was published.

The new Grid is based on the same two motivational scales as the earlier version. But the authors added a new dimension. They analyzed the positive (+) and negative (−) attitudes and traits within a particular Grid style. There is also a zero, or neutral, point that falls in the middle of the plus-minus scale.

The new Grid gives us more information about different leader styles than was available in the original Grid. Let's look, for example, at the 1,9 style. Blake and Mouton state: "In this Grid style a person wants to gain the love and approval of others. That is the consuming interest in life. To suffer rejection is the most feared result, because it demonstrates to a 1,9-oriented person that one is not only unworthy of love, but even more damaging, he or she is the target of unwantedness by others."[5] In our earlier examples, Chief Davis used a 1,9 style and gave in to the men's demand on the parade. Using the revised grid, we can better appreciate the considerations Davis

Leadership Styles ◀ 19

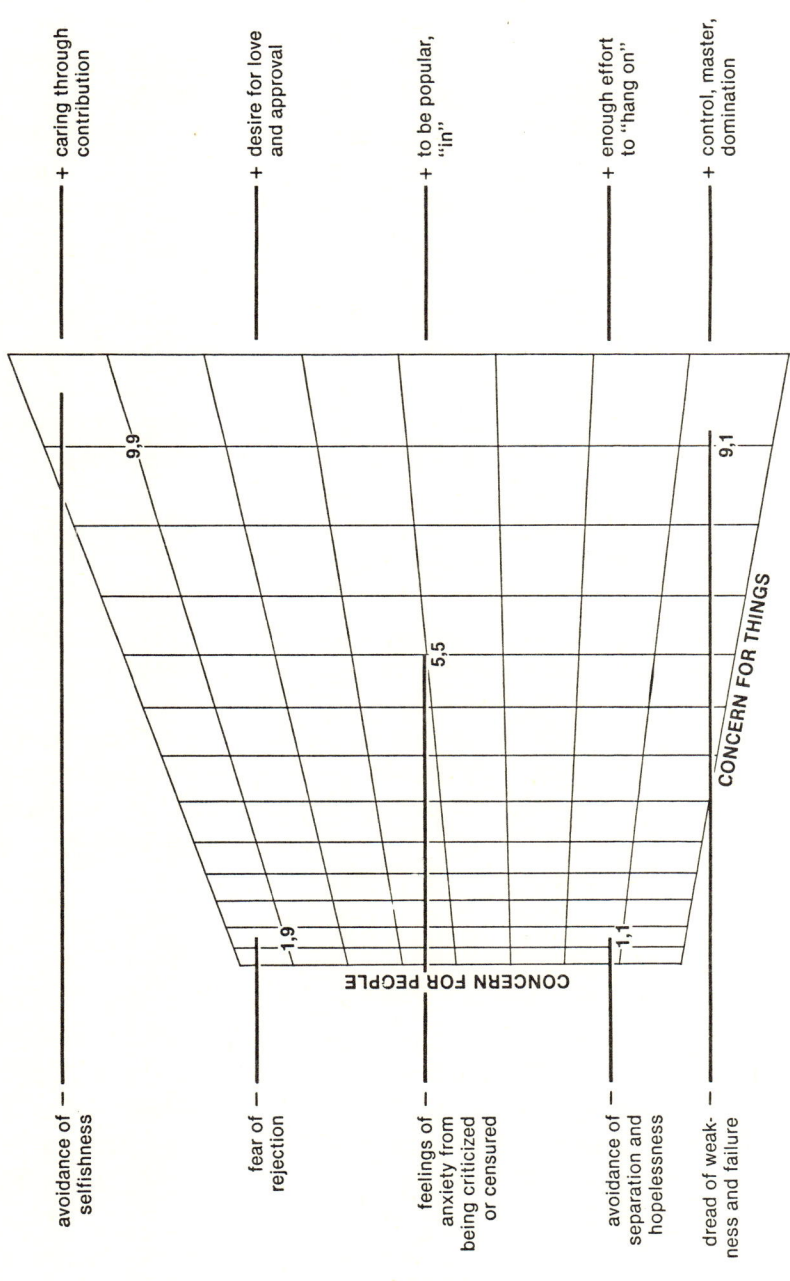

Figure 1.2

took in coming to that decision. The positive attitude represents Davis's desire to be well liked and respected by his firefighters; the negative is that being liked was more important than repairing the apparatus. This is how a 1,9 leader might indeed act.

There are probably a few 1,1-oriented fire officers, though we hope there aren't too many around these days. These officers use a poor overall management style. They are not willing to work at achieving good relationships. They believe that they cannot reach successful outcomes because people are basically underachievers. People are people—nothing you can do will change them. The result is that their plus (+) motivation becomes doing nothing more than is absolutely necessary, just "hanging on."[6] On the negative side, they employ actions or attitudes that can be interpreted as disinterest, thus losing the respect of their personnel.

As for the 9,9 profile, the most desirable leadership style in the new Grid, Blake and Mouton say:

Here we find that the positive pole (+) involves the pull of achieving important life goals and outcomes with and through others which in turn aids them to be happy and effective as well. This motivation has sometimes been referred to as egotistic altruism, enlightened self-interest or self-fulfillment. The negative pole (−) relates to avoiding defeat such as occurs when a person views a situation as one in which there can be no gain and no possibility of making a contribution.[7]

The Grid in Realistic Terms

The Blake and Mouton Grid is useful because it's an understandable model with which to analyze leadership. Nevertheless, some people don't think it's a fully effective model. Some critics argue that the Grid explains a complex topic in much too simple terms. They also feel that identifications such as 1,9 and 9,9 are too easily created and force evaluators to think only in those terms.

As a fire officer, you should keep in mind that the authors of the Grid never said that all managers must fit into the Grid's specific leadership styles. Instead, they identified two very realistic concerns that affect a leader's actions; one concern is people and the other is production and outcomes. Given these two concerns, Blake and Mouton explain some obvious leadership traits to help us understand how the Grid works. Realistically, 1 and 9 on the Grid represent minimums and maximums. Between those two points, there's a lot of room to look at a leader's style.

Also remember that there will be times when you will lead your firefighters more by circumstance than by self-determination. On the fireground, especially when there is a possible life loss at stake, outcomes take precedence over blind concern for your firefighters. I'm not saying that you should behave as Chief Grey did, oblivious to the unnecessary risks he made his firefighters take. But if you have civilians trapped in a tenement, you have no choice but to attempt every conceivable rescue method. Some rescue methods will certainly be risky to your firefighters; nevertheless, those risks are part of their job. And it's part of your job to order your firefighters to take risks when civilian lives are in jeopardy and rescue is possible. To decide whether your decisions affecting people and outcomes are reasonable, you must look at them in terms of your ultimate responsibilities.

You may find that the Grid is more useful for leadership behavior that you initiate with your officers and firefighters away from the fire scene. You make more decisions away from the fireground than you do on it. So you can work harder on improving your leadership style when you are not under the tension of an emergency situation. As long as you are not afraid to be honest with yourself, you can think about your strong and weak points as a leader. What you know will work with your people, you will want to build on and reinforce; what fails to work, you will want to change and try again a different way. The Grid is a realistic aid as you look at your leadership style, and it offers a better chance for positive change in your style than does leadership by chance and without direction.

WHAT SHOULD YOU STRIVE TO ACHIEVE?

We know that a 9,9 leader is the one who stands the best chance of succeeding in all his responsibilities. He successfully meets his goals and objectives with the support and optimal effort of his subordinates. I believe that these effective leadership characteristics can be developed in all of us, contrary to the feelings of some that a 9,9–oriented result is "pie in the sky." An officer who knows how to attain his goals and earn the respect and compliance of his subordinates is the kind of leader the fire service needs. A good officer is a good officer— regardless of whether he directs a paid or a volunteer force. Good leadership transcends such distinctions.

Strive in every way to be a 9,9 officer. Draw on the best abilities your firefighters have to offer, keep an open mind and reasonable perspective, and manage by forethought instead of crisis. Through participation and interaction comes agreement and disagreement. But the final outcome is resolution, usually in the best interests of the fire department. Your leadership actions will greatly affect what those resolutions are to be.

Situational Leadership Theory

Paul Hersey and Kenneth H. Blanchard designed the Situational Leadership theory as a component of their book, *Management of Organizational Behavior*.[8] Just as in using the Blake and Mouton Grid, you can apply meaning to any situation when one person leads another. And Situational Leadership has a lot of practical use for volunteer officers who want to improve their leadership abilities. This is especially true in this day and age when some in the fire service criticize the profession for not being more modern but holding fast to the parochial, traditional ways of years past.

Situational Leadership is based on specific research. First, it says that the demands of a leader's environment dictate different leadership styles if that leader is to be successful. A leader who has a rigid style and doesn't adapt to the vastly different behaviors of his subordinates is going to have a tough time being an effective leader. Second, Situational Leadership emphasizes the leader's behavior in relation to his followers. The follower's role is important because the follower either accepts or rejects the leader and because followers can affect a leader's personal power. Third, a leader adapts to his subordinates' ways depending on their "maturity" levels. Situational Leadership presents maturity in a task-related sense. That is, you look at those you manage in terms of how they perform a specific task. The way you supervise and direct is a way of understanding how to best lead people with varied maturity levels. Some people may need you to teach the task performance in the correct way as well as encourage them to succeed when they try it. Others may show higher degrees of maturity and be able to perform essential tasks with a minimum of supervision and support from a leader.

Volunteers work closely in the fire department. They train together, fight fires together, and participate in other community services representing the fire department together. Yet they, as individuals, have different levels of competency maturity. Therefore, their chief and officers must understand that they have to relate differently to each individual firefighter from the way they relate to firefighters as a collective group.

When they use Situational Leadership, leaders' actions are based on two specific things: task behavior and relationship behavior. As the leader decides a subordinate's maturity level in task-relevant terms, the leader either increases or decreases both his task and his relationship behavior with the subordinate.

For example, a chief may see that one of his new lieutenants is very good at sizing up the fire scene when he rolls in as first due. But the lieutenant may need to be a little more forceful when he gives orders based on his sizing up. With these facts as background, the chief knows that he does not need to sit down with the lieutenant and teach him what factors he should consider when arriving on the scene. Thus the chief can decrease his task behavior—he can spend less time talking about sizing up a fire scene and more time explaining about how to give orders to others—much more than he would with rank-and-file volunteers. He may further encourage the lieutenant to be more forceful in giving orders because he, the chief, has strong confidence in what the lieutenant is telling his firefighters to do. Here the chief is increasing his relationship behavior by encouraging. As that lieutenant becomes more "mature," the chief can eventually decrease his relationship behavior.

When the fire chief relates to his assistant chief, the situation is different. By the time a volunteer has reached the level of assistant chief, he has usually proven that he thoroughly knows his department's fireground operations and tactics, as well as that he has good rapport with the other volunteers. Part of his role as the second in command is to learn the finer points of being chief of department.

Because the chief and assistant chief usually know each other well and have spent many years together in the department, the chief realizes that there is not a great deal he needs to teach his second in command about being a fire officer. Nor does he need to motivate him to any great extent. Therefore, the chief uses minimal task and relationship behavior when he works with his assistant. It isn't necessary to look over the assistant chief's shoulder all the time.

THE SITUATIONAL LEADERSHIP THEORY MODEL

Hersey and Blanchard have designed a formal situational leadership structure that suggests what leadership styles will have the greatest probability for success, based on the task and relationship behavior maturity level of the subordinate.

Figure 1.3 shows a curvilinear function used in Situational Leadership theory. To use the model, you plot a vertical line from the determined maturity level of the subordinate until it

Leadership Styles

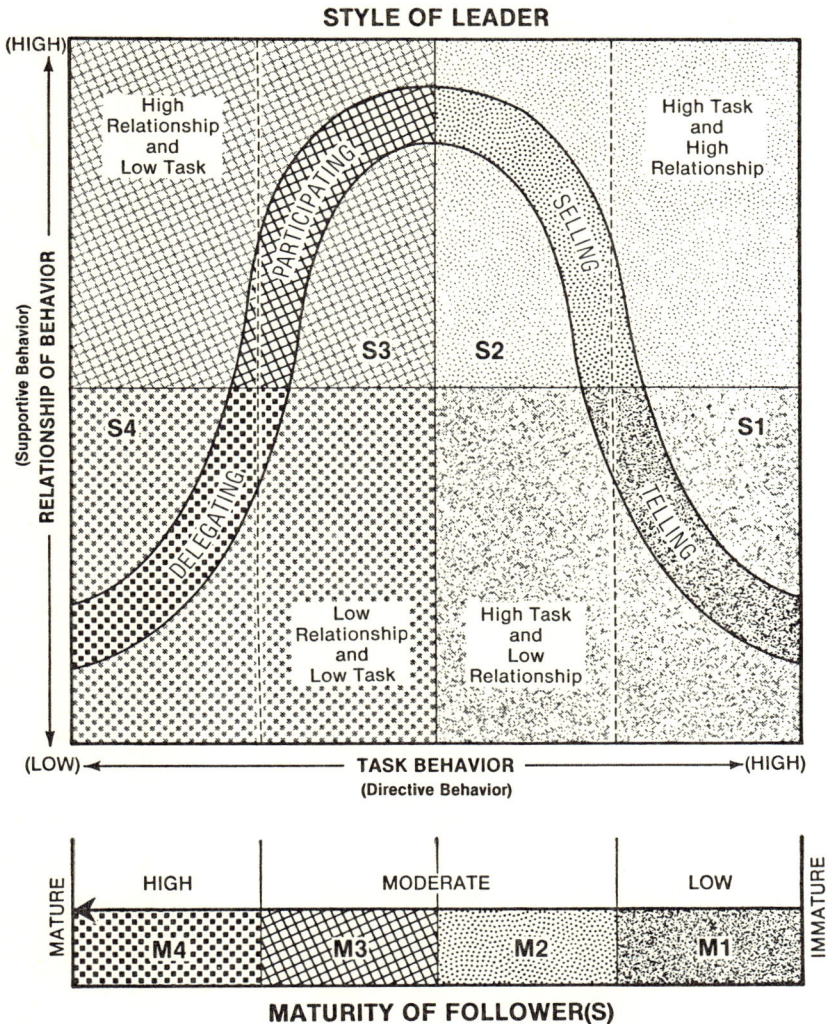

© Copyright 1977 Paul Hersey and Kenneth H. Blanchard. All rights reserved.

Figure 1.3

meets the leadership curve. This identifies what leadership style is most effective to use. The four quadrants identify four distinct leadership styles:

Quadrant 1—High task/low relationship
Quadrant 2—High task/high relationship
Quadrant 3—High relationship/low task
Quadrant 4—Low relationship/low task

Selection of an effective leadership style from the four styles identified is based on the maturity level of the subordinate. M1 indicates a low maturity level; because of this, the subordinate needs a leader who has a high task/low relationship style. M2 reflects a low to moderate maturity level; use a high task/high relationship style. M3 is for maturity levels from moderate to high and works best with a high relationship/low task leadership style. M4 represents a high maturity level and calls for a low relationship/low task leadership style.

The correlation between maturity level and suggested leadership style is based on the high probability of that particular leadership style's being successful. Hersey and Blanchard do not say that a leader cannot use another style; however, the probability of success with other styles will be lower.

Another interesting part of Situational Leadership involves the kind of relationship behavior a leader exhibits. For example,

- High task/low relationship behavior is also called "telling"; the emphasis is on the leader doing most of the talking. He clarifies for the subordinate what, when, where, and how.
- High task/high relationship behavior is also called "selling"; the leader still does most of the communicating, but also encourages the subordinate to ask "why" he should be doing something.
- High relationship/low task is also called "participating"; the degree of two-way communication between subordinate and leader gets stronger because task maturity is higher. The subordinate has a lot of ability to perform the task.
- Low relationship/low task behavior is called "delegating"; it is evi-

denced when the leader realizes his subordinate needs little teaching to perform the task, as well as minimal encouragement. He trusts the subordinate to work on his own.

Relationship of Situation Leadership Theory to Fire Department Management

A high task/low relationship leadership style is useful when you are dealing with rank-and-file firefighters. You might have the most contact with them on the fireground or during training. You are evaluating and reacting to the task maturity level that each man demonstrates. Of course you talk with your firefighters during social hours at the firehouse. But the officer's role as leader is strongest as fireground commander.

There are exceptions. One exception might occur when a lieutenant is identifying a firefighter who has shown high task maturity. Perhaps nominations for line office are coming up. Believing that a particular firefighter has definite leadership potential, the lieutenant may personally encourage this firefighter to keep up the good work and consider running for line office. The degree of relationship behavior the lieutenant shows is higher than would usually be shown with a rank-and-file firefighter.

The relationship between a chief and his first-line company officers, usually lieutenants, works well when the chief leads them with high task/high relationship style. Since these young officers still have much to learn as fireground officers (highlighted by their usually being the first officers at the scene), they must be led with a high task style. At the same time, the chief should realize that their motivation and enthusiasm will affect how well they perform as first-line officers. A good chief, therefore, tries to both teach and encourage them to a high degree.

A high relationship/low task leadership style is appropriate when a chief officer works with his middle-level officers, usually captains and deputy chiefs, in a volunteer department. These officers have a lot of fireground experience and usually demonstrate high task maturity as firefighters. Thus the emphasis on task is minimal. But the chief should use a high relationship style with these men. Middle-level officers are at a plateau in their volunteer careers. They are knowledgeable, yet their goals of becoming chiefs of department may seem rather far away. This being so, their behavior is very important. The fire chief will use their talents best by leading them through a high relationship/low task leadership style.

The final example of Situational Leadership's relevance to volunteer firefighters is when a chief uses a low relationship/low task leadership style with his second in command, the assistant chief. What the assistant chief has to learn is the finer points of being the person in charge. When the chief lets his assistant "run his own show" from time to time, be it at the fireground or during a training session, he is leading with this particular leadership style. Whatever the assistant chief needs to learn, he will get through direct experience in task areas. He usually doesn't need to be motivated to any significant degree.

SITUATIONAL LEADERSHIP THEORY IN REALISTIC TERMS

The above examples of leadership effectiveness with subordinates are not cast in concrete. There will certainly be times when you will lead particular volunteers, be they firefighter or fire officer, in ways not consistent with the examples just described. That is the beauty of Situational Leadership. The authors make it clear that a leader is effective because he perceives the particular maturity level, both task and relationship oriented, of the subordinate. As a result, the fire officer makes the most of his one-to-one communication with his subordinates in order to make a proper assessment of where each man is and how he should be led.

Keep in mind that the fire department is a paramilitary/emergency service operation. It has to operate in a formal fashion to run effectively. That is, a high task/low relationship leadership style is appropriate because firefighters operate under combat conditions and great stress. They must effectively react to orders. There is no opportunity to sit down and discuss engine and truck company operations as though one had all the time in the world. Time is of the essence. Behavior must be quick and responsive.

When an officer meets and talks with his firefighters off the ground, however, he can use appropriate leadership styles other than "telling." Now he can better adapt to the subordinate's task maturity level and use an appropriate leadership style.

Counterproductive Leadership Styles

At times, leaders tend to have all the weaknesses manifested in classic leadership molds. Some of the ineffective managerial styles show up in fire officers, and our discussion of them should serve as a reminder that such styles are counterproductive to good management.

THE "KNOW-IT-ALL" OFFICER

This fire chief has made it to the top of the ladder, and now he has the right to be egotistic and authoritarian. There is nothing that he doesn't know, administrative or operational, and he communicates with his subordinates in one direction: down.

His rigid attitude is the exact opposite of that of the leader who adapts to his personnel. The know-it-all's rigidity is far from the attitude found in the Grid and in Situational Leadership. Good leadership is a dream with this kind of officer. He will never realize the full potential of his firefighters.

THE "EVERYBODY'S BUDDY" OFFICER

This fellow is the embodiment of the 1,9 manager. It's not that he doesn't know his firefighting; he does. But his desire to be a popular officer overrides his need to exert authority whether his decisions are popular or not. This is not uncommon in the volunteer service; being well liked can be important for a volunteer, especially one who aspires to officer status. Nevertheless, the desire to be popular can and will stand in the way of being the good officer he may well have become.

The "Panic Button" Officer

This officer is usually knowledgeable. His behavior as a "panic button" officer is usually the result of his managing by crisis. He lacks the foresight to do long-range planning and foresee problems as they are developing in his department. He tends to act only in crises, and this hurts his efficiency as a good leader.

I mention these three leadership styles for two reasons: (1) Although they seem rather classic and are not that common, they do occur and should be avoided; and (2) I present them to show that good leadership can be achieved and that the need for good leadership becomes more obvious when we look at poor styles.

Participatory Management

In simple terms, participatory management means making the most of what all officers have to offer. It means making the final decisions, but decisions that are arrived at through participation, disagreement, agreement, and eventual resolution with your fellow officers. An effective fire chief solicits the opinions, thoughts, and suggestions of his officers. They can actively participate in the decision-making process and can have the satisfaction of knowing that they had a role in a positive outcome.

Participatory management also helps a chief's image with his officers. It is a strong preventive action against becoming a know-it-all chief and can develop that essential degree of humility found in all good leaders. Each of us has something to learn from others, even if they are our subordinates. The measure of a good officer is one who makes the most of his own skills and the skills of his followers. A good leader must do this if he is to reach his goal of running an efficient, professional fire department.

Final Thoughts

Born leaders sometimes happen along, just as sports stars sometimes capture the public's attention with their natural talents and their precision, timing, and accuracy. But not all good leaders are born leaders; a willing person can learn to be a strong leader if the ability and desire are there. Good leaders in all professional ranks work actively to improve their leadership skills and managerial proficiency. The fire service should be no exception. Professionalism transcends paid and volunteer ranks. An effective leader *is* a professional leader.

Notes

1. Robert R. Blake and Jane S. Mouton, *The Managerial Grid* (1964).
2. Ibid.
3. Ibid.
4. Robert R. Blake and Jane S. Mouton, "What's New with the Grid?" *Training and Development Journal*, May 1978, p. 3. See also their *The New Managerial Grid* (Houston: Gruf, 1978).
5. Ibid., p. 4.
6. Ibid.
7. Ibid.
8. Paul Hersey and Kenneth H. Blanchard, *Management of Organizational Behavior: Utilizing Human Resources* (Englewood Cliffs, NJ: Prentice-Hall).

The price for not planning is more than we should be willing to pay. We must develop the ability to clearly understand our objectives and set attainable goals. Failing to plan is planning to fail.
—WILLIAM ANDERSON, ASSISTANT CHIEF,
GREENSBURG VOLUNTEER
FIRE DEPARTMENT,
GREENSBURG, PENNSYLVANIA

2 / *Planning*

Every volunteer fire officer comes into his officer's job excited about new ideas and challenges that will improve fire department effectiveness. The new lieutenant wants to start an intensive training program for his station members. He wants his station to be the best in the department. The new fire chief has been anxiously waiting for the appropriate time to push a sprinkler ordinance for all commercial establishments in town.

If you're a new chief, start planning now for what you want to accomplish six months or even a year from now. If you're a junior officer thinking about what you will do as chief a few years from now, the planning techniques and skills I discuss in this chapter will be immensely valuable to you now and when you rise to the rank of chief officer.

Whatever the goal, it's incumbent on the planner to design a systematic, step-by-step plan. Certain tasks have to be accomplished, and by certain dates. Officers must assign responsibilities to the individuals who will perform these tasks. In essence, the planner must consider every conceivable factor and plan how to handle it.

But before you start making those plans, let's examine the important parts of planning with which you should be familiar. These items are the skeleton of planning; your particular plan is the muscle and tissue.

Identifying Major Project Tasks

The goal sometimes looks awesome, and you wonder where you will begin. You'll find that it's far less frustrating when you identify the primary tasks that can help you reach your project goal. It's much like renovating an old home—it seems such a huge job. But renovating one part at a time is manageable—and it's the sensible approach. In essence, each job becomes a primary task. You may begin by replacing plaster with dry wall. Then convert the one-car garage into a workroom. After that, you may add two more breakers to your electrical system and put in ten more switches and outlets. The tasks continue until the renovation is complete.

Reducing a goal to its specific tasks is essential to successful planning. It really lets you see what you have to do.

Delegating Responsibilities

Experience has taught us that a good manager delegates responsibilities. You, the chief, cannot do everything yourself. You have senior and junior officers, as well as firefighters, and these people are competent enough to assume some of the work load. And they should do so, because every member of the fire department has a vested interest in the department's success.

By delegating duties you become an effective planner in a variety of ways. First, you speed up the anticipated accomplishment date for the project because a number of tasks are being worked on at the same time. Second, you earn the respect of your firefighters by letting them take on some responsibility. When it's their job to get the tasks finished, their pride and desire about finishing become important. You are spreading the wealth and letting others have a part in the project. Third, you are living up to your role as an able manager. Yes, managers *do* work. But they also are expected to use the best skills of their subordinates, to give them projects and tasks to follow through on.

You don't need to do it all yourself. Assign work to others, and the end result will be a job well done that everyone can be proud of.

Performance Objectives for All Tasks

One point I discuss later in this book (in "The Training Function" chapter) is performance-based objectives. I mention them here because these same objectives are necessary in planning.

When you delegate assignments to members of the department, their work effort must be toward some measurable end. If you cannot measure whether a task is completed, then you're planning on shaky ground. It should be clear what is to be accomplished.

Stating the end result is different from stating an activity. Using the example of the house renovation again saying, "I'm going to rewire the new receptacles," is an activity. But saying, "All old receptacles and switches will be replaced and operational by six weeks from today," states the end result of all the tasks that accomplished it. Planning tasks toward an end result is best done with clear objectives of what is to be accomplished each step of the way.

Completion Dates

Stating performance objectives that are measurable is only part of the job. Another essential is to have anticipated completion dates, and to make dates that are realistic and achievable.

The best-planned objectives can be unmet when no one thinks about when they should be met. When you provide realistic completion dates, the individuals responsible for carrying out your objectives have a time frame in which to work. When they develop an action plan for a particular task, they know their priorities; they know what they're going to do and how long it should take to do it.

Just as your major goal must have a projected completion date, so should every phase of an action plan. It adds a necessary "time" discipline to the project.

Don't worry about delays because delays are going to happen. There may be a delay in securing some materials. Or it may be a delay in getting an OK from certain municipal officials. The nice thing about completion dates for objectives or action plans is that they can be adjusted. Sure, a delay can keep you from meeting your deadline. But at least you had a deadline! When you have a delay, simply readjust the anticipated completion dates affected.

Working with Outside Groups

The sample planning project at the end of this chapter shows how objectives can be planned in conjunction with the individuals or organizations outside the fire department that are working with you. At this point, though, just be aware that you'll probably be working with outside groups.

Because you're an officer and your plans often include municipal officials, expect them to have certain tasks too. The decision you have to make is whether to leave the responsibility for those tasks with your subordinates, working along with the officials, or with the officials themselves. This ends up being a judgment call. You have to decide how committed (or not committed) these officials are to your project and its effect on the community.

For example, you may be very enthusiastic about using the National Fire Protection Association's (NFPA's) Learn Not to Burn fire prevention curriculum. (By the way, as an educational model for youngsters, there isn't a better one.) You have spoken to a number of elementary school teachers, and they're evenly split between using and not using the curriculum. So you take your case to the superintendent of schools, and you receive very strong support along with a verbal commitment to incorporate the curriculum at all elementary school levels.

Since you're promoting fire prevention in your community,

the schools are only one part of the project and based on what I said earlier about delegating responsibility, it's probably safe to leave the responsibility for the fire prevention curriculum with the school superintendent. He's the person who has the authority to force change in that area.

It's your job, however, to explain to the superintendent how that task is part of a major objective to increase the number of ongoing fire prevention programs in the community. The school superintendent needs to understand what you want to accomplish, your action plans for it, when it should be finished, and by what standard or measure you will decide whether the objective was met. Getting this information across demonstrates to the superintendent that you have actually practiced objective setting and action planning.

We all understand that any fire protection/prevention improvement plan directly affects the whole community. Working with people outside the fire department is inevitable. The degree to which these people can help you achieve your objective will be affected by how well you've planned. The better you plan, the more they can help you.

Maintaining Records

A cardinal rule in planning is to maintain detailed and up-to-date records of all events and actions concerning the objective. This is even more important when you delegate certain parts of the objective's action plan to subordinates. They are accountable for results. And they become your primary means of tracking accomplishments, delays, or handicaps toward meeting the objective.

Insist on the practice of maintaining accurate records right from the start. Have your subordinates file progress reports to you on a regular basis, such as weekly or biweekly. These reports should be detailed, clearly stating what was accomplished and what was not. Concerning problems that arose, the responsible person should write comments on what caused the problem and how he expects to solve it.

Planning

The Actual Process

The best way to learn objective setting and action planning skills is to use them. This part of the chapter shows you how — step by step. I use a hypothetical yet realistic objective for a volunteer fire department and work it through from start to completion. It's as close as you can get to the real thing.

The skills involved are the ones you'll use as an officer. What I'm presenting is a guide. It's up to you to take the skills I've discussed and use them.

Objective

The Smithville Volunteer Fire Department will design, develop, and implement a modern communication system for dispatching fire and rescue services. Funding for the project will be $100,000 through a grant from federal and state agencies. There will be a time period of seven months to complete the project and install the system.

The criterion for successful project completion will be the dispatching of fire and rescue personnel resulting in an average reduced response time of one half minute or better over present response time (from alerting to arrival at the scene) for a period of six months after the system becomes operational.

This statement meets the requirements of an objective. First, the audience has been identified: the Smithville Volunteer Fire Department. Second, the department's action or behavior will be "to design, develop, and implement a modern communication system for dispatching fire and rescue services." Third, there is a list of conditions under which this project is to take place, as well as a specific amount of money available to finance the project. Fourth, the project has a time limit for completion: seven months. And fifth, there is a criterion on which to judge whether the new communication system is making a difference: By using it, there should be a significant reduction in response time of fire/rescue units.

When you're specific, it's much easier to begin the action planning phase of the project.

Action Planning

Producing an action plan for an objective is what gives that objective its measure of reality. Something is going to happen: installing and operating a new communication system. The action plan is your road map for reaching your objective. When you have more than one objective, each objective needs an action plan of its own, with dates for its accomplishment. In this example, however, we build our action plan for our one central objective as follows:

1. A master plan of the project must be written and must serve as the reference guide for all project activities, planning, and outcomes. A project task force is to write the plan, under the chairmanship of the chief of department. The final master plan is to be ready for presentation by two months from project start date.
2. The master plan must contain the following information:
    a. Application requirements, testing methods and procedures, and related criteria for the job of fire/rescue communication dispatcher.
    b. Research on currently operating communication systems that serve volunteer fire and rescue emergency personnel. Data and findings to substantiate that the proposed communication system will reduce response time of emergency units by a significant degree.
    c. A public education program to inform and educate the community on the services of the new system and how they should use it.
    d. A communication system design that meets both existing fire and rescue needs and anticipated future demands as determined from the Smithville community master plan and the county master plan.
    e. Design for a mutual-aid response system with neighboring communities for the immediate dispatching of volunteer fire/rescue units to supplement Smithville units if needed.
3. All committees are to write a draft report on their findings and recommendations and submit it to the project task force by (specific date).

Planning ◀ 39

4. Task force review and recommendations of all committee reports are to be submitted by (specific date).
5. Committees are to modify and rewrite all reports, based on task force review, and to submit final typed reports to chief of department by (specific date).
6. Presentation of the project master plan is to go to funding agencies and municipal officials for acceptance or rejection. Accomplish by (specific date).
7. If the master plan is accepted, the task force must write specifications for those companies bidding on the project by (specific date).
8. Solicitation of bids for the project are to be published; receipt of bids is to be accepted no later than (specific date).
9. Task force review of bids is to be completed by (specific date).
10. Acceptable bidders are to make oral presentations before task force. All presentations are to be completed by (specific date).
11. Task force is to make its recommendations to funding agencies and municipal officials on bidder selection no later than (specific date).
12. Contract award winner is to be officially notified by (specific date).
13. New communication system is to be installed and operational no later than (specific date).

THE COMMITTEE ACTION PLAN

We can take the action planning phase one step further. Every committee must prepare a list of activities for its members that will result in the committees' report for the task force report and master plan. For example: *A public education program to inform and educate the community on the services of the new system and how it should be used.*

1. Chief designates public education program committee members; committee chairman is to serve as public information officer for the project. Accomplish by (specific date).
2. Chief and public education committee meet to clarify responsibilities and tasks. Accomplish by (specific date).

3. Chief and chairman/public information officer meet to clarify the chairman's role:
    a. Coordinate committee work.
    b. Serve as assistant liaison with community groups, the press, and outside agencies on the project.
    c. Design a schedule for informing community residents of the project.
4. Committee chairman assigns specific tasks to committee members. Accomplish by (specific date).
5. Draft reports are due back to chairman by (specific date).
6. Chairman reviews reports no later than (specific date).
7. Modifications are to be made and chairman is to submit final public education program committee report to project task force by (specific date).

There has to be some documentation of all events. The project record sheet shown in Figure 2.1 is a planning record sample. Its value is that it identifies not only what the objective is and who has responsibility for it but all the extenuating circumstances that either hindered or helped the action plan. Should the fire department decide to stop work on the project at some point and begin again at a later date, it will have a written record of where the project stopped and what still lies ahead in order to finish it.

Figure 2.2 is the statement of the actual action plan, step by step. It's a continuous reference on what has happened, what is happening, and what will happen and on when all tasks were, are, and will be done.

Some people use a time-line chart when they plan. You can plot the anticipated progression of each activity in terms of other activities and when the entire project will be completed. Figure 2.3 shows a time-line chart of the proposed new communication system. You can see that some activities can go on at the same time.

Objective 1:

Coordination/Responsibility Assigned to: _____

Action Plan:
    Project accomplishment date:_____
    Actual accomplishment date:_____

    Outcome:

    Evaluation:

    Recommendations:

    Issues Pending:

    Standard of Measurement:

Figure 2.1 Smithville Volunteer Fire Department Project: New F/R Communication System

Action Plan: Completion Date

1. _____
   _____
   _____
   _____
   _____   _____

2. _____
   _____
   _____
   _____
   _____   _____

3. _____
   _____
   _____
   _____
   _____   _____

4. _____
   _____
   _____
   _____
   _____   _____

5. _____
   _____
   _____
   _____
   _____   _____

Figure 2.2 Step-by-Step Action Plan

Planning ◀ 43

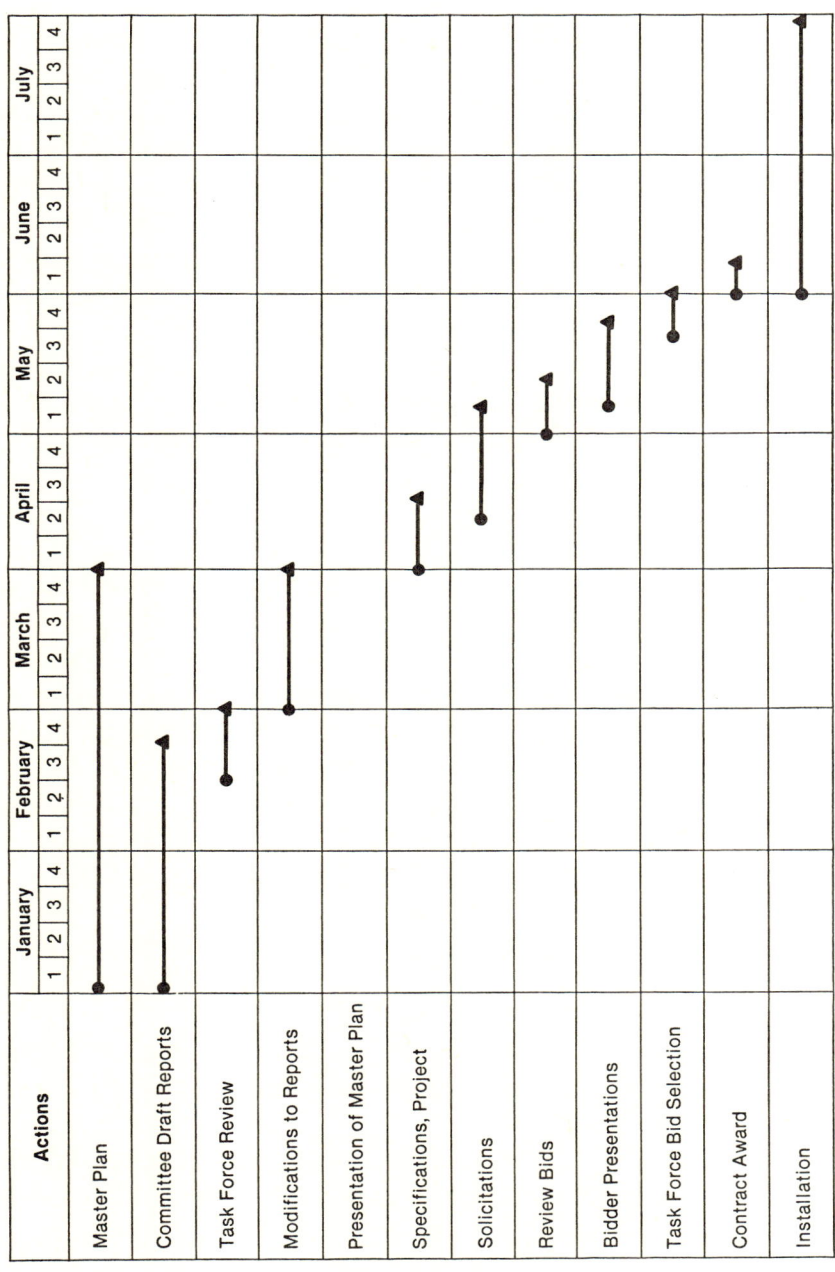

Figure 2.3 Time-Line Chart

44 ▶ The Volunteer Firefighters' Management Book

Is It Worth It?

I have just taken a project—installing and operating a new fire and rescue communication system—and have shown the objective setting and action planning you have to do to make that project a reality. At times, however, the best-laid plans fail. What happened? Why did it fail? Was there something missing among the objectives of the project? Did someone forget to plan an important activity? Maybe. It could also be that the odds for the project's success were low right from the beginning.

It's possible to predict project outcomes and as a result really see whether the commitment of time, money, and human resources is worth the price of success or failure.

FORCE FIELD ANALYSIS

An effective method for analyzing the probability of project/planning success is called Force Field Analysis. Through this method, the planner or planning group evaluates the forces supporting the objective against the forces opposed to it. We can design a purely hypothetical situation where Force Field Analysis will reveal a low probability of success.

First, we plot each force or circumstance on a chart that measures "supports" or "opposes" on a scale of 1 to 5 in which 1 is the minimum and 5 the maximum for both positive and negative factors (See Figure 2.4).

Here's the list of circumstances that make up the rankings shown in Figure 2.4.

Circumstance 1. The Smithville fire chief, the Smithville rescue squad chief, and twenty volunteers from both organizations support the plan.
RANKING = +1. *Explanation:* You have leaders who support the plan, but because the numbers are small, the ranking is not that strong.

Circumstance 2. There are 240 firefighters and rescue vol-

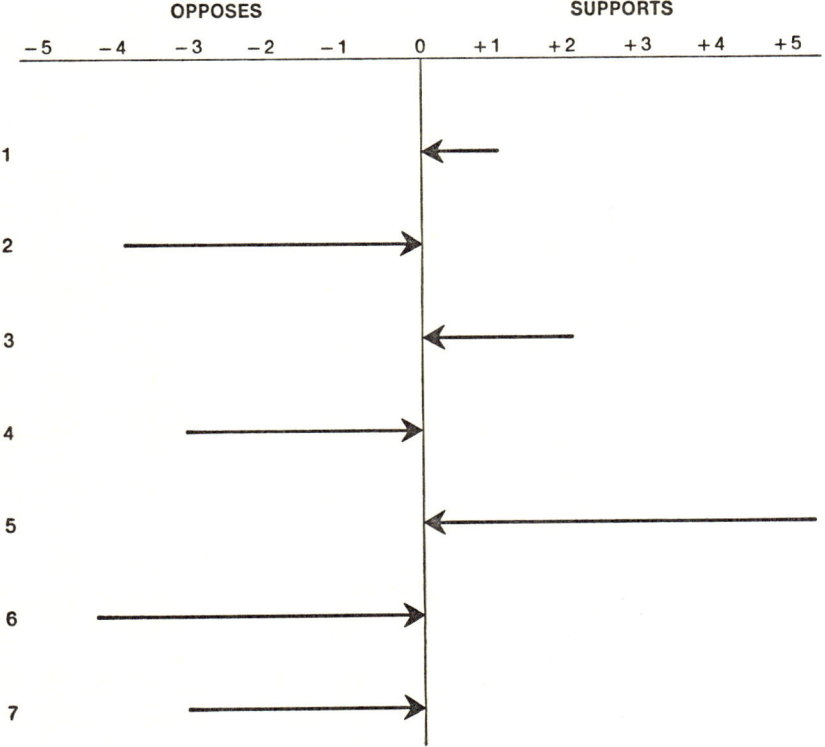

Figure 2.4 Force Field Analysis for
Smithville Communication Project

unteers in Smithville. The remaining members of both organizations are opposed to the plan.
RANKING = −4. *Explanation:* The number of volunteers in Smithville who oppose the plan is overwhelming and it earns a strong negative ranking.

Circumstance 3. The mayor and police chief also have come out in support of the plan.
RANKING = +2. *Explanation:* The ranking is a little higher than in circumstance 1 because two municipal leaders support the plan. But read on.

Circumstance 4. The local police officer's labor association views the project as stripping the police of some present responsibilities. It may affect their future bargaining power when

contract negotiations resume. They are unanimously opposed.
RANKING = −3. *Explanation:* Labor often carries more weight than management. And because the policemen have a strong local union, they are a definite opposing force.

Circumstance 5. The total cost of the project will come from a joint federal/state grant.
RANKING = +5. *Explanation:* Everybody is worried about money these days. But not in this case. Full funding from other agencies is a big plus.

Circumstance 6. The salaries, benefits, and training of the new civilian dispatchers will be borne by the taxpayers of Smithville. The town's civic organizations are adamantly opposed to any increase in municipal costs that they must finance and have so stated in numerous public forums.
RANKING = −4. *Explanation:* The public may want a new communication system, but they would rather give it up than pay higher taxes to support municipal costs.

Circumstance 7. The Smithville fire chief's tenure will expire during the project period. His successor does not favor the plan and has so stated publicly.
RANKING = −3. *Explanation:* It speaks for itself.

What the results of these examples show is that, with the exception of project costs during installation being covered by grant money, the forces opposing the new communication plan considerably outnumber the supporting forces. It's important to have support from organizational and municipal leaders. But the absence of backing from the rank and file of those organizations is already stacking the cards against the plan.

This example of Force Field Analysis is purely hypothetical. It's very possible that you will have different circumstances in which the supporting factors strongly outweigh the opposing ones. In that case, the odds are very good that the project can be a success.

If you were the Smithville chief, knowing that there was

strong opposition to the plan, what could you do to meet your objective? The obvious answer would be to try to reduce the degree or number of opposing factors. Some solutions:

1. Schedule meetings between fire/rescue leaders and membership to discuss openly why the leaders favor the new system and its potential value to the fire department, rescue squad, and community.
2. Schedule meetings with the police officers' association leaders to resolve their concern about their labor position being jeopardized.
3. Schedule meetings between the fire chief and rescue squad chief and civic leaders to demonstrate that the incurred costs to the taxpayers will be small in relation to other municipal expenses.

It's conceivable that you'll remove some opposing factors and yet no significant change occurs. If that happens, it's probably best to scrap the project until some future date when you can organize and run a strong public relations campaign to explain your objective to everyone.

Force Field Analysis is a simple yet valuable analysis tool. It is useful in any planning process in which people have a sincere commitment to succeed yet know all realities of the situation. And you don't need to get a lot of people together to practice this method. All that's needed is one person, a piece of paper and pencil, and an objective viewpoint.

Planning is not that complex a task. Yet having strong planning skills and abilities is a valuable resource in any professional and personal venture. Being an effective leader is important. But there must be a direction in which to lead. Because every group, formal or informal, usually has some collective goal, every group needs a plan.

As an officer, you are the captain of the ship. Your skill as an effective planner is one of the best safeguards against your ship's (your command's) wandering with neither direction nor purpose. Work hard to cultivate good planning practices. The payoff will be beneficial to your responsibilities as an officer now and in the future.

Public relations is not an on-off proposition. It is a continuous job, one that requires attention and planning. More important, first impressions are critical and the public expects more from a firefighter than it does from other people. The bottom line is that there is no better choice than a fire department that gives prompt, effective, and understanding service. You rarely get a second chance to make a good impression.

—WILLIAM PECK, FORMER CHIEF,
EAST BRUNSWICK INDEPENDENT
FIRE COMPANY, EAST BRUNSWICK, NEW JERSEY

3 / *Public Relations*

Volunteer fire departments are traditionally proud of the job they do for the public. Volunteer firefighters always put forth their best effort. But like all people, their frustration level can reach the boiling point on some occasions. It can happen when the community's local ruling body stands in the way of a progressive attempt to improve the level of fire protection for the town. Or when citizens are ambivalent about or ungrateful for the service they receive. Or when there is poor or even no cooperation between the fire department and other municipal services in the town or county, and this lack of cooperation hinders the volunteers. Or when volunteers work hour after hour at a fire, through a freezing night in winter or in the blasting heat of summer, only to find that the local papers the next day give more press coverage to the new triplets born in the town. Some people in the news business seem unaware that a major fire is a true test of a firefighter's stamina and courage.

The public comes to you on two occasions: when they have a complaint and when they need your assistance. It's up to you as a fire officer not to exist in the public mind for these two reasons only. Be aggressive, not timid. Educate people so that they understand what they *should* understand. Make them work for you and with you. To do this, you have to conduct one first-rate public relations campaign.

Public Relations

Must all good things come from within the department? Even with a solid body of personnel and a smooth-running internal system, aren't there a number of outside factors that can ruin all your efforts to build an efficient, proud fire department? The answer to this last question is a definite *Yes*! An uncooperative and unresponsive local government, a public that takes its fire protection for granted, and media that fail to credit firefighters for a job well done can ruin morale a lot faster than it took to build that high-motivation level.

The governmental structure, the community, the media — take them all seriously as forces that can help or hinder the fire department. The fire chief has a pivotal role in this phase of fire department management. When it comes to meeting with and educating local officials, the only person they want to deal with is the fire chief. When the newspaper reporters want a statement on what happened at a serious fire, it's the chief they seek out. When citizens in town have a gripe to make or a compliment to hand out, they usually want to go right to the top of the chain of command. All these outside groups will seek you out. The way you choose to handle them can mean the difference between making them your allies or your adversaries. And when they become "your" allies, they become the allies of all the members of your department.

It's a large task to tackle. You won't find it easy or something that you can do quickly. But when you set your mind on a practical approach to working with your local government officials, the members of the community, other civic and public service organizations in town, and the media, you are laying the groundwork for the future — for the time when everyone in your community will know more than just that "the fire department is there." They will understand your dedication to your work, the enormous responsibilities you have, the limitations under which you work, the services you deliver, and the unrepayable benefits everyone gets from his volunteer firefighters.

Local Government

Local political ruling bodies are organized in different ways. In some communities, there's a mayor, a business administrator, and town councillors. Other places have a county executive or county manager. You also come across boards of freeholders, who govern beyond a municipality and operate under a county or regional structure in which there is no county executive. Whatever the design of the ruling political body, these politicians can be tremendous allies of the fire department. It all depends on your approach.

The line officers, the bench officers, and the fire company trustees or board of fire commissioners should collectively decide how to work with local government. Take the time to evaluate the present relations between the department and local government thoroughly. What have those relations been like to date? Have they been weak, strong, or moderate? Have relations improved or worsened with each new political administration, depending on the entering attitude of the newly elected political leader(s)? Who has generally made the first step in establishing relations with the new mayor and town council: you or the new politician? Have town leaders seen the fire department in action other than at fires? Has there ever been an official committee in the fire department to handle public relations with media, the community, and local leaders?

This is a mouthful of questions. But you should ask yourself these questions as you lay out a plan to improve cooperation with local officials. Let's assume, for instance, that you have convened a meeting to discuss political relations and the group decides that more needs to be actively done to educate the mayor, town councillors, or county executive. You are ready to act—but what should you do? Here are some ways to improve your standing in the community with these politicians.

Special Training

If you're planning a special training exercise, such as an LPG (Liquefied Petroleum Gas) or LNG (Liquid Nitrogen Gas) fire, invite the mayor and selected town councillors to attend. Let them see at first hand the danger firefighters are exposed to at a moment's notice when they are trying to extinguish or control a fire. Your guests may surprise you. They may request your permission to put on full turnout gear and go in on the line with some experienced firefighters. As long as they will accept the responsibility, why not let them get a feeling of what it's really like? In the end, they will value your service to the community even more.

If you decide to invite guests, you must carefully plan the training exercise from start to finish. To begin with, have all firefighters organized into teams, headed by officers, so that everyone is clear about where he belongs throughout the training. Randomly picking out people to go in on the fire demonstrates poor preparation and organization, and your guests and other civilian bystanders will notice it.

Consider all safety factors at your training exercise. I assume that all your trainings are planned from a safety standpoint, and you never needlessly allow any dangerous conditions to exist. At the same time, you are in the spotlight when outsiders are present. If they are there to watch your men and your operation in action, doublecheck everything. This is the last place to have an unnecessary accident.

In any event, don't hesitate to invite guests to fire company training exercises occasionally. And take advantage of this public relations effort when you hold special trainings that you may schedule only every one or two years.

Fund Drives

Money makes all organizations go in this day and age. Though we join the fire department to be volunteer firefighters, we still need money to exist: to purchase and repair apparatus, to replace old turnout gear, to cover registration fees at advanced training programs, to maintain stationhouses and grounds, and so on. If your department does not receive a set percentage of the municipal or county tax money for fire prevention and protection, or if you receive only a nominal fee from the town for the protection of municipal property, then you are at the mercy of solicitations to make ends meet.

A fund drive is an experience unto itself, as you well know. You meet the irate and ungrateful resident as well as the accommodating one. You meet residents living in $100,000 homes who come forth with fifty cents for a fire department fund-drive donation. It runs the whole gamut. The point is that the public will typically take advantage of tough economic times to shortchange you on your end. Some people just don't know that fire protection services are provided by an all-volunteer department that isn't funded by municipal taxation. And some people have a "wishful thinking" attitude that "it's always someone else's house that catches fire; my house won't burn." In their eyes, this attitude justifies giving a minimal contribution, if anything at all.

This is all true, and we know it is. So why not invite an interested town councillor to accompany one of your officers on a fund-drive call, either through the residential or commercial end of town? He does not necessarily have to be introduced as your officer goes from house to house or business to business. What is important is that the public official get a firsthand look at the typical frustrations of trying to raise funds.

If you decide to try this technique, pick a politician you already know. He or she should know a lot about the fire department. And you should know how that person really views the department in relation to other public service groups in town. You want a supporter on this trip.

On the other hand, you may want a borderline member whose ambivalence toward fire department financing may swing in your favor if he or she can see the problems up front. Remember, though, that this can be risky because the individual may not see things your way. But it's worth a consideration.

In addition, have your politician spend some time with you and your fund-drive chairman, learning how your fund-drive operation works. Only with a clear conception of how a financing program operates can a politician appreciate the difficulties you encounter every year.

Prefire Planning

If your fire protection response area has commercial structures (and a growing number of volunteer departments have this situation as the rate of industrialization grows in this country), you have probably "prefire" planned some or all of the older and newly built commercial buildings. Consider inviting the mayor or a member of the town fathers to accompany you and your men on a prefire planning tour of a building in town.

All this is a learning process for you, for your other officers, and for your firefighters. It can also be a lesson for your guests. They will see that your fire suppression tactics are not based on reaction to emergency alone. They will also see your interest as an officer to be as aware as possible of potential firefighting hazards in your community, and how you are preparing for them.

When these politicians witness your thoroughness in fire protection planning for the town, it's easier for them to support you at some later date when the fire department might be accused of not doing anything except responding to calls—of not preparing for fire dangers. Close contact with your local governing body helps build your image.

Community Events

At least once a year, fire departments hold community gatherings to promote the fire company. Most departments generally hold some public event—it may be an open house—during fire prevention week in October. Yes, these kinds of activities certainly give the community resident the chance to meet their volunteers and learn a little bit about them.

Make sure that the mayor, the town administrator, and town councillors attend these events. Most of them are elected officials, and so they will want to take advantage of such events to market themselves with their constituents.

FIRE CHIEFS ASSOCIATION/PUBLIC SAFETY MEETINGS

It isn't unusual to find towns or municipalities served by more than one volunteer fire department. In fact, some towns are protected by as many as five independent fire companies. As these towns grew in size, residents organized new fire departments in addition to the existing ones. Residents formed their own group, wrote their own charter (probably with considerable argument with the founding fire department), and designated their own geographical area of fire protection. There is considerable room for argument for and against this kind of fire protection system, varying opinions on how good or bad it is. Nevertheless, it exists.

The chiefs of these departments meet periodically as a formal body to discuss and plan fire protection responsibilities for the town as well as better coordination of fire protection efforts. Sometimes, the chief of police is a member of this board, as is the president or chief of the rescue squad, depending on whether the group is called a "town fire chiefs association" or a "town public safety association."

If you are a chief officer in your department and a representative of the group, it is in the best interests of your department and the fire protection system of the town to have some local politicians sit in as nonparticipatory guests at some of your meetings. Of course, if you know in advance of some sensitive issues that will be discussed at a particular meeting, don't schedule that meeting to be the one that has outsiders present. When you are discussing a community fire issue, such as a campaign to increase smoke-detector use in residential dwellings, it may be an ideal time to have a town councillor sit in on the meeting. For all you know, he or she might have some excellent thoughts on ways to promote that idea in the community. In fact, a program for fire prevention may just need that extra push from the town council.

A Parting of the Ways

I have suggested methods of improving your image with local leaders, but there comes a time to draw the line and attend to your business without outsiders. For example, don't invite local politicians to your department's business meetings. These times are for the membership to participate in the decision-making process of department administration. Discussions can get heated and controversial. These meetings should be for fire department members only.

The same goes for meetings of the line, bench, and trustees. Matters discussed here are privileged and confidential, even to the point where general membership is not informed unless the chief, president, and trustees feel it is in membership's best interests to know.

After a major fire, many chiefs hold critiques with their firefighters and discuss what happened at the fire—what was successful and what was poor from a tactics and fire suppression perspective. Local officials may be glad to know that postfire discussions are held to keep the department from making the same mistakes twice and in order to know what will work in practice as well as in theory. But the critiques are no place for outsiders, whether they be politicians or members of the press. An officer must be able to raise his voice when he wants to, or pay special compliments at meetings, without having outsiders present. Certain things should remain behind closed doors, and a postfire discussion is one of those times.

A smart officer will not discuss a fireground operation with a city official in front of civilian bystanders or members of the media. If the official and the fire officer disagree about how the fire was fought, the chief should not have to justify his actions right at the fire scene to a politician who doesn't understand firefighting tactics and strategies. At a big fire, emotions are high. This is the place to fight the fire, not to argue with the mayor. The best philosophy is to leave any points of contention to a personal discussion between you and the politician *after* the fire is completely under control and all units have cleared the scene. Then you can tear each other's hair out.

State and Federal Politicians

Local politicians are the ones most visible to you. You talk to them often. But they are not the only politicians you must identify as important to fire department interests. Every state in the union has a legislative body made up of state senators and assemblymen. At some time or another, there will be political issues affecting your and every other volunteer fire department in the state. It may have to do with volunteers using emergency lights on their vehicles. Or it may be a question of whether volunteers will be eligible for full benefits under the Federal Public Safety Officer Benefits Program if they die during a fire.

Your state assemblyman lives in your town or in the surrounding area, and so he can meet with you and other fire officers. All fire department officers must take the initiative and arrange meetings with state legislators. When a particular bill is up for debate by the senate or assembly, make it clear to the politician what your stand is and why you have reached that decision.

Many politicians don't understand the unique problems of the volunteer service, not to mention their knowing nothing about firefighting. They cannot represent your best interests if they don't know your feelings, pro or con, on certain matters under debate in the state legislature.

Also, some politicians take a cavalier attitude that political matters concerning volunteer firefighters are not that important. Maybe they're not—to them. But you can be sure that they are important to the community. It's the people in the community who will benefit from improvements in your system. So constantly remind these politicians that you and your men are community-minded citizens as well as volunteer firefighters.

And you are voters. Collectively, you and other volunteers throughout the state constitute a number of votes that cannot be ignored.

Don't feel ashamed or embarrassed about being aggressive. Huge corporations pay large salaries to their representatives in Washington to lobby the corporation's interests with U.S. senators and congressmen. Other public interest groups, such as antiabortion and consumers union coalitions, are constantly telling their state and national legislators that their interest group should not be ignored because they have blocs of voters behind them. Why should the volunteer fire service be any different?

As an officer in the department, you have ideas about improving the level of fire protection in your community. Be firm and make your concerns known to your state and federal representatives. Be ready to give a push at the right time, when it's in your best interests. Remember, politicians cannot know how you feel about what's important—and what isn't—unless you tell them.

Media Relations

One of the quickest ways to get information to large numbers of people is through the media. Whether it be through television, radio, newspapers, or magazines, organizations that have something to say to the people do it through the media.

Within the fire service, numerous publications keep firefighters abreast of the latest technical and administrative trends in the field. These publications are excellent references for fire service personnel. But most of them are available only within the field. Someone from the outside who wants to learn about firefighting cannot buy these publications on the newsstand. They have to know some firefighters who are subscribers who will lend them the publications. That's not the firefighters' best media outlet.

Newspapers, radio, and television traditionally cover fire department events such as a major blaze, labor disputes, and pension problems. The volunteer service has been fortunate in that its special problems usually get publicized. An example is kicking off a fund drive and having the local paper do a piece on it so people will be anticipating firefighters coming to their homes. Newspapers, television, and radio publicize only certain fire department events, however, and they publicize only what the media staff decides to tell the public. Another way of saying it is that these journalists publicize only what *they* think is important unless the fire chief steps forward and assumes some responsibility. The media cannot print what they don't know.

The media can be terrific promoters for the fire department. On the other hand, they can set back months, even years, of progress with one bad story. The volunteer service should use the media to educate the public on what volunteer firefighters do, why they do it, and how they hope to do it better. Let's take a look at some ways to accomplish this.

Newspaper Coverage

As soon as it comes over the wire that there is a major fire in town, a reporter who covers the fire and police desk will pick it up on his scanner and be on his way. Fires make news because property is destroyed, victims sometimes die, and firefighters take extreme risks. People always stop and watch fires because the element of danger is exciting.

The way the reporter gets his information about the fire is important. If a bystander tells him that it took the fire department ten minutes to arrive, when in fact it took four minutes, the department is put on the defensive. It has to get the right information across to alter a negative opinion in the public's mind that the department doesn't do its job very well.

An even better example is a chief in charge of a fire's decision to let a pesticide fire continue to burn. He knows that letting the fire free burn may present less of a risk than letting other toxic chemicals form as by-products if water is applied to the fire. The reporter doesn't know this. If the chief doesn't say anything, the next edition's story may generate unfair publicity for the fire department for letting a dangerous fire burn. Don't blame the reporter; he just didn't understand the firefighting strategy employed, and no one explained it to him.

Establishing a good working relationship with the press is important. It helps get the correct information passed on to the public. How, then, do you do it?

Find out which reporters from your local papers generally cover fires and get in contact with them. Let them know that you are interested in press coverage that will be of value to the fire department. This holds true for all fire department activities, not just fires.

Once you establish this important communication process, these reporters will start coming directly to you at the fire scene. For that matter, make them aware that you are the official spokesman for all fire department matters on the fireground unless another individual is specifically designated. All nonfire-related matters will be handled by the president of the fire department. Unless other members are officially authorized to make public statements, all quotes and comments should come from you or the president.

The press will respect you for clarifying all procedures for printing direct statements from fire department officials. It makes for a relationship with fewer problems; important issues are not left to conjecture or opinion.

Use discretion in deciding when to talk to reporters at a fire. You are there to do a job. At the same time, the press can be of help. If there is a break in operations during which you can take just a few moments to brief reporters on the status of the fire, they will appreciate it. Also, set aside some time to brief the press on what basically happened: the cause of the fire (if determined at that time), conditions that forced certain firefighting tactics, a report on injured firefighters, and so on. It's all part of letting the press know that you have a vested interest in what is printed about the fire department. You want it to be correct.

Always maintain your composure with press personnel.

There may be a time when a reporter tries to put you on the firing line with a leading question. You realize the implications of the question and that it is leading to a bad reflection on the department. Whether the interpretation of the issue is correct or not, keep a cool head. Don't lose your temper. When you keep your wits about you, you answer questions properly and don't have to agonize later, wishing you hadn't said what you did in haste.

Working with the fire department president, seek out the press to help you publicize a particular concern or state of affairs. For example, some commercial enterprises in your town may be uncooperative during your fund drive. They occupy a large space of property and run profitable businesses, but they could not care less that your department depends on contributed money to provide adequate fire protection.

The press is the conduit whereby citizens in town can learn of this problem. They have a right to know that particular retailers want their business but are not concerned enough with their safety, should a fire occur in their stores. The best way the public can learn about this is through the newspaper. It reaches a large audience in a short time.

Reaction to such a story can go two ways. The public's response may be minimal or nothing at all. Or a group of citizens may publicly express their concern with the situation. They may choose to write to the "letters to the editor" section of the paper or even choose to stop doing business with a particular store. They may contact the mayor and town council to see if some pressure can be put on certain store managers. Finally, they may contact you and ask what they can individually do to assist, to help reach a solution favorable to the fire department.

The press can help do all this, and more. Lay a foundation for support and cooperation among you, the fire department president, and the newspaper professionals. When you get in a pinch, the press will come through for you.

Radio and Television

Just a word about radio and television. The same principles for sound cooperation apply with these communicators as do with newspaper reporters. Treat radio and television personnel with courtesy, clarify how they will get their information from you, and be a professional with them.

If you have a complaint with a radio, television, or press statement about the department, find out the source of the statement before you raise the roof. You can really be embarrassed if confidential information becomes public and you start hollering, only to find out that one of your firefighters said more than he should have to a media representative. One incident like that, and everything you have worked for in media relations can be ruined.

Fire Service Publications and Professional Events

Publicity within your avocational or occupational field is just as valuable as communicating with the rest of the public. People in our field earn reputations and recognition because of publicity in fire service publications.

Many publications serve the American firefighter: *Fire Engineering, Fire Service Today, Fire Chief, Western Fire Journal, Firehouse, International Fire Chief, Fire Journal, Minnesota Fire Chief*, and many others. These publications present a lot of interesting information, ranging from the latest philosophies on special fireground tactics and strategies to contemporary issues in administration and management for all fire chiefs.

Editors and publishers eagerly want articles from fire people in the field in order to make their publications effective. A new idea that has been successful is of value to others across the country. In fact, this is something that the fire service has always prided itself on: welcoming new ideas and practices that others can use.

Don't be afraid of submitting articles that are newsworthy to some of the magazines. When you share professional ideas, you help other fire departments, and your department is better known in fire service circles. It is a form of public relations within the field that is just as important as getting the message out to the public.

Along these lines, fire chiefs and administrators meet at national meetings and conferences where they share experiences, learn new concepts in leadership and fire suppression, and discover the latest and most efficient equipment on the market. The International Association of Fire Chiefs Annual Conference, Fire Department Instructor's Conference, California Fire Chiefs Annual Conference, and New York State Fire Chiefs Association Annual Conference are some of the largest and best-attended meetings for fire officers.

Fire service personnel come to these conferences to learn. They also come to promote some of the things their department is doing. It is, again, a public relations effort. Participating in fire service organizations and attending conferences, when practical, are great experiences. Many volunteer chiefs have heightened their department's image through some national organization. Your local papers will be eager to pick up the information if you serve, for instance, on the firefighter health and safety committee of a recognized fire service association. When that information gets out to the townspeople, it improves your image and the image of your department.

Educating the Community

Emergency service and public safety personnel, whether they are paid workers or volunteers, have traditionally been taken for granted. The typical citizen believes that help will come if his house catches fire, he suffers a serious accident, or his television and stereo system are stolen. Until such time as this individual needs the assistance of the fire department, rescue squad, or police department, he remains largely ignorant about how these organizations operate and how effectively they render service.

I don't expect every citizen to know how a volunteer fire department operates. That's your job. Nevertheless, citizens who know a little about what you do for them and some of the difficulties you face in accomplishing that job are better able to help you. That help could be during a fund drive. Or it may happen when you're having trouble with the town council in getting municipal property zoned for a new fire station.

Regardless of the situation, don't expect the public to come to you. You have to get the message out to them, to educate them. It's no easy job to overcome ignorance, misconceptions, and a belief that the fire department is and always will be there, that the public should expect you to volunteer your time and effort just because they live there.

LET THEM KNOW YOU ARE VOLUNTEERS

In rural parts of the country where communities are small and everyone knows one another, the volunteer fire chief and his firefighters have an advantage. Everyone in town knows they are volunteers. It has been that way since the community was founded and will likely remain that way for a good while to come. The fire load in this kind of town is not great enough to warrant a full-time department staff, nor could the town's budget afford the cost.

This situation, though, is not the prevailing case anymore. Our country is still growing by leaps and bounds. Communities double in size as shopping centers and business offices take the place of open space. Some towns still maintain all-volunteer departments, while others make the transition to some career personnel in the form of a paid chief and paid drivers.

In these communities, it is not unusual for new residents to be "immigrants" from the big city. They are escaping the urban jungle and are trying to live the American dream with a beautiful home, two cars, and color television. They bring with them their perceptions of what living in the city was like and the services they received there. One such service was fire protection from a fully paid fire department. If someone asks them who provides fire protection in your town they will likely say that the firefighters in town are paid and municipal taxes maintain fire stations, equipment, and apparatus, not to mention training and other costs.

Their ideas could not be farther from the truth. Your firefighters are all volunteers, you purchase and maintain your own apparatus, and you may depend on fund-raising activities (sometimes combined with funds from the municipal budget, but not always) for your finances. You must correct these misunderstandings or they will prove continually frustrating. If citizens believe that their firefighters get paid to fight fires, then they will be uncooperative when your firefighters knock on their doors canvassing for money. Someone may also complain that you were late getting to his home for a fire call, believing that your firefighters are always at the station instead of at their homes or their places of business, as volunteers generally are.

There are ways of clearing up these misconceptions and properly informing as many residents as possible about their volunteer fire department. First, use your connections with the local newspaper and take out a full-page ad. It's expensive, but it's worth the cost. People read newspapers, and large ads attract attention. Write the ad in a positive tone, expressing gratitude for the support that most residents have given to the department over the years. This is also your opportunity to set the record straight. Make it clear that all fire protection is provided by volunteers who unselfishly give their time and effort to the community. Make it clear that the community must support the fire department financially if it is to maintain a high level of service with decent equipment and apparatus.

Second, include a flyer inside the fund-drive envelopes citizens use to send in their contributions. Most volunteer departments do this. Design your flyer so that you have attractive and attention-grabbing promotional inserts. You may want to give some tips on fire safety in the home or state the essential and immediate things to do in case of a fire. The point is this: Don't overlook this opportunity to educate people. Citizens *do* read this material; maybe it is read by more people than you imagine.

Third, organize a Public Relations Committee within the department. As chief, you can oversee the operation of the committee and guide the members in the right direction. The best avenues of communication for this group are through the political, religious, civic, and social organizations in the community. By getting permission to speak to these organizations at their weekly or monthly meetings, you'll get your message out the door. Actually, the key behind this approach is the public relations officer. I'll discuss his duties a little later in this chapter.

Fourth, display your apparatus at community events such as county fairs and Memorial Day and Independence Day community gatherings. Ask for volunteers to do this, yet be selective on who gets chosen. These individuals should be well spoken and make a decent appearance. When children scamper to climb on the fire engines, their parents often talk with the volunteers exhibiting the apparatus. The parents can learn a great deal about their fire protection services if you choose the right volunteers to explain the work. It is an easy, comfortable opportunity to communicate with the public.

Finally, don't neglect to schedule fire department–sponsored events. The public can find out a great deal about your work at an open house and during national fire prevention week activities.

"You Owe Me Protection"

Every volunteer, at one time or another, has met the abusive, arrogant citizen. This individual probably knows that you're a volunteer because he or she has been a resident of the community for years and knows that the community's firefighters are not career personnel. This person is simply rude.

A volunteer may meet this person during fund drives when the resident calls the firefighter "one of those bums who drinks beer and makes a lot of noise with his siren." Or when firefighters respond to the individual's home on a fire call, and the person doesn't even thank them for their effort, even though they made a good stop on the fire. Volunteers also run into this person when they're driving to the fire station on a call. The arrogant citizen knows that there is someone behind him responding to an emergency. He can see the headlights and the flashing blue light in his rear-view mirror. Yet he never considers pulling over to the shoulder of the road, allowing the volunteer to pass him without crossing into other lanes of traffic.

Can you do anything to change this kind of mentality? Not really. There will always be a few people who have rigid attitudes, and it would probably take an act of God to change them. For this reason, you have a very important duty as fire officer to make new volunteers aware that someday, sometime, they will run into one of these characters. What should they do?

Unless they are physically assaulted, tell your firefighters to remain calm and simply listen to it as it goes "in one ear and out the other." If they want to try to discuss the fire department with a negative-minded citizen while canvassing for contributions, for instance, they should not be discouraged from doing so. They should be warned, however, that this tends to be useless. It's simply better to be pleasant, thank the person for his or her time, and walk away.

The abusive or rude person has an ax to grind. If it's not with you or your firefighters, then it will be with someone else. Your volunteers give of their time, above and beyond the call. They shouldn't be subjected to undeserving ridicule and abuse. But if it's unavoidable, they should try their best to ignore it.

The Public Relations Officer

Volunteer fire departments always have a chief, president, fund-drive chairman, corresponding secretary, treasurer, and trustees, among other officers. One important role often neglected is public relations. Few volunteer departments assign the public relations task to a particular firefighter or group of firefighters. Public relations matters are generally handled by the chief or the president.

Don't misunderstand. There is absolutely nothing wrong or irregular in a situation where the chief or the president handles public relations responsibilities. Earlier in this chapter I talked about an officer's role in building good public relations with local officials and members of the media. An officer is a manager of the fire department. But a chief officer manages many jobs. If it's not budgeting for new equipment, then it's planning for a meeting with the mayor on an improved communication dispatching system for the department. Whatever the reason, the chief is certain to be in the middle of different fire department business.

A sign of successful management at a chief's level is when the chief assigns important tasks to responsible people. He not only delegates authority and responsibility in an effective fashion but he encounters firefighters who are motivated and can do a good job. One job that can be assigned to a dependable firefighter is that of public relations officer for the fire department. This firefighter can handle a number of responsibilities.

1. He can take care of many of the speaking engagements arranged through the political, civic, religious, and social groups of the community. If the chief cannot attend, the public relations officer usually can.
2. I spoke earlier about an officer talking to and briefing members of the press at a fire. If the public relations officer is not coordinating fire control and extinguishment but is waiting on standby should another call come in, he can take some of the strain off of the chief, letting him tend to the business of fireground command.
3. The public relations officer is a suitable fire department member to coordinate with the public and private school systems to teach schoolchildren about the fire department's work in fire prevention. Many fire departments that have career personnel now assign firefighters to the position of public fire education specialist. And they do more than just educate the public about the danger of fire and the need for better preventative measures at home. A good deal of it is public relations.
4. When firefighters are confronted with the "arrogant" citizen, the public relations officer is an excellent person to handle a follow-up meeting with this person. It's the public relations officer's job to explain the fire department's role to people who misunderstand it.

Pick one of your most able firefighters to do this important job. Public relations work is excellent preparation for learning to deal more effectively with people in general, and firefighters do a lot of that. Your public relations officer can really help you and can give you the time to address the equally pressing matters you're responsible for.

Fire Department Community Events

Throughout our lifetimes, we learn that the average person prefers to receive rather than to give. It contradicts that old rule about "it's better to give than to receive," yet it's true. Asking someone to give you something can make that person defensive. He wants to know what he'll get in return. On the other hand, people are more relaxed and friendly when something is either given to them or done for them.

This philosophy holds true when a volunteer fire department sets out to teach the community what a fine job the volunteers do. When the volunteer asks community residents for money, whether it is for raffling something at the fair or running a fund drive, it's sort of a one-way street. Unlike the volunteer, who knows that any one of the town's residents may need help in a fire emergency at one time or another, the citizen finds himself putting out money but not immediately needing the services of the fire department. He doesn't necessarily see it as an investment in future protection.

The fire department can do a few favors for the community, beyond putting out fires. It counterbalances the situation in which the resident is always the giver and makes him the recipient. What favors can you and your men do? Here are a few suggestions.

OPEN HOUSE

Many fire departments sponsor some kind of open house during fire prevention week. Aside from providing presents and entertainment for children, during an open house the town resident gets a chance to see how his fire department donation is being used.

Plan a number of educational experiences for the adults. Make small presentations that explain how to contact the fire department in an emergency; the purposes of the equipment you maintain and operate; your response system; fire prevention tips for the home, such as exit drills in the home and selection and placement of exits; and other items. Also, provide some facts and figures showing the man-hours that volunteers spend on fire response, training, nonfirefighting duties, and others. This kind of information clearly demonstrates how much time you and your personnel donate to the town.

This is also a chance to promote a membership drive. Some guests are bound to ask questions about becoming a member of the fire department, and you should be prepared to answer them.

Open house is not an event that must take place only once a year during fire prevention week. You may want to hold an open house as often as three times a year. Some fire department members may criticize this and say, "Open house only draws the same people each time, the ones who value their firefighters. Those who don't care never show up at all." That may be so. At the same time, residents move away, and new ones move in to take their place. New town members can become new allies and supporters of the volunteer fire department if they can get the word from you instead of some apathetic neighbor. If they just missed the open house that's held only once a year, you won't have a chance to talk to the new folks for another year.

CPR Training

In volunteer fire departments where firefighters also administer prehospital emergency care through basic and/or advanced life-support techniques, such as those provided by emergency medical technicians and paramedics, there is one excellent activity that is beneficial to the entire public. It is Cardio-Pulmonary Resuscitation Training (CPR).

Doctors have labeled heart disease as the number-one disease afflicting Americans. Part of the American Heart Association's effort to reduce the staggering figures of death and disablement from heart disease has been to teach people that the initial four minutes are critical when someone has suffered a cardiac arrest. In the last half-dozen years, millions of Americans have been trained in what to do between the time that they come upon a cardiac arrest victim and qualified medical assistance arrives on the scene. "What to do" is keeping blood flowing to the brain with fresh oxygen that must be artificially transported through CPR.

The fire department is a logical place to hold periodic CPR training courses for the public. The fire department is an emergency services provider with which the public identifies when an emergency occurs more so than they do with the police. CPR training courses provide great visibility for you and your firefighters.

Blood Pressure Screening

You can also assist residents and win their support through a blood pressure screening program. As is the case with CPR training, your firefighters can do this for the public only if they have training and certification as emergency medical technicians or paramedics. If your town is served by both a volunteer fire department and a rescue squad, then sponsor this program as a joint project between your two organizations.

By holding blood pressure screening clinics in a joint fire department/rescue squad sponsorship, you can (1) have the public come to the firehouse and meet the firefighters, (2) educate the public on the services provided by the rescue squad, (3) help reinforce the fact that both organizations are manned and staffed by volunteers, (4) provide a public health service to town citizens, and (5) enhance your image for the time when a fund drive starts again.

FIRE PREVENTION SEMINARS

The Christmas holiday season and the winter months in general are peak times for residential fires. Causes for these fires include overloaded electrical circuits from Christmas tree lights, chimney flues, home heating oil burners, and many others. For this reason, a great way to educate the public, promote the fire department's service to the community, and reduce fire hazards in the home is through a holiday season fire prevention seminar or presentation. You can hold it at a high school auditorium or other public gathering place. Citizens will appreciate this kind of seminar immensely, and they will remember what they learned at it.

Educating the community means taking the initiative. You have to take the first step to meet the people, instead of expecting them to understand your situation and your needs. Just as you ask the public to give during a fund drive and other money-raising events, so must you reciprocate and serve them in different ways. Your leadership in this aspect of community relations is important, and your volunteers should make a commitment to it.

Working with Other Public Employees

The working relationship between the fire department and other county or municipal divisions is important. Life in the fire department can be somewhat frustrating when a chief and his firefighters are in constant disagreement, and sometimes open warfare, with other civil servants. Who are these other public employees, and why is their assistance valuable to the fire department? What are your responsibilities as an officer in making these working agreements positive and cooperative?

The Police Department

When the fire department responds to an emergency, the police usually respond as well. Both are essential emergency service providers with different and distinct jobs. Because both usually work together, each must understand the other's roles and responsibilities.

An example that illustrates this point is dispatching fire department volunteers in parts of New York and New Jersey. On the north and south shores of Long Island, New York, volunteers provide almost total community fire protection. Some of the towns have their own uniformed dispatchers and communication systems to receive emergency calls and alert the volunteers to respond. It is not necessarily a function of the Nassau or Suffolk County Police Department. If you cross the river into New Jersey, however, and head into the central part of the state where volunteers make up the majority of firefighters, the situation is different. In some central New Jersey townships, all telephone calls for the fire department first go through police headquarters. The police dispatcher on duty at the time of the call then alerts the fire department.

Now, the fire chief must coordinate with the chief of police to ensure the quickest, most accurate alerting of his volunteers from police headquarters. He and the police chief must agree on the following:

- Who gets alerted first when a fire call comes in: a police patrol car or the volunteers?
- At the fire scene (particularly a major fire), who is the ultimate commander of all emergency operations: the fire chief or a ranking police officer?
- What is the police chief's attitude on essential dispatcher skills and abilities for a police officer answering fire telephone calls? Will these police officers be specially trained in gathering vital information from an excited person phoning in a fire?
- If responding firefighters actually see an arsonist, do they have the right to detain that individual forcibly until a police officer arrives at the scene?

If a state's emergency statutes do not specify who has the final word at a fire scene but leaves it up to the municipality to resolve, then some procedure must be set pretty fast. Otherwise, there will be chaos amid disaster. Here is an example of what can happen.

Your town has a six-lane interstate highway that passes through a heavily commercialized area with densely populated residential sections close to the highway. The commercial areas are shopping centers, smaller retail businesses, and fast-food chain restaurants. During the afternoon on a weekend summer day when people are both shopping and traveling in great numbers, an 18-wheel tanker transporting liquefied petroleum blows a front tire on the highway. In the ensuing accident, the tanker ends up on its side with one of the sides of the tank ruptured. While the fire department and police are en route, the escaping LPG vapors ignite and the tank begins to burn.

The first arriving engine's officer discovers that the tanker has been burning for two or three minutes. Fully aware that immediate water application must be started to prevent a BLEVE (Boiling Liquid Expanding Vapor Explosion), he also realizes the imminent danger to people within a 2,000- to 3,000-foot radius should the tanker explode, let alone any other catastrophes that may occur from flying shrapnel.

This is the point at which a conflict may occur. Deciding that the life hazard is too great, the fire officer orders all his men to evacuate. He also pulls the ranking police officer aside and requests that the following be done:

- All traffic heading toward the accident site in any direction be detoured at a two-mile point from the site
- All existing traffic already within the two-mile area be turned around immediately
- All available police vehicles with public address systems become operational and begin to evacuate any civilians and community residents within a 3,000-foot radius of the burning tank
- All hospitals within a fifteen-mile radius be notified to prepare for a mass disaster
- All neighboring communities' firefighting and rescue personnel be placed on alert and standing by at their stations

- One township police officer be placed at the fire station of each neighboring (bordering) town to direct that fire apparatus to any fires should there be a BLEVE.

As the fire officer finishes stating his requests, the police officer says, "Wait a minute. Who gave you the authority to give these orders? I only carry out orders from the chief of police." This is the worst time to find out who has authority and who does not. If the delay in getting those orders carried out results in the unnecessary death or injury of a single civilian, somebody is (and should be) in a great deal of trouble and has a lot of questions to answer. The time to coordinate and work with the police chief is *before* the emergency occurs.

Also, you as a fire officer should know what your powers of authority are in your town and state. Cooperating with the chief of police does not mean relinquishing emergency scene control simply to be agreeable. It's possible that the police chief may try to take advantage of the situation by virtue of his being a paid official and your being a volunteer. Don't allow this to happen. Be clear about, and never relinquish, your authority.

The Road Department

Employees of the road department assist the fire department in varied ways, and they are good friends to have. When it snows, they're the ones to plow out each fire station and make sure that there's as little snow as possible on the pad outside the bay doors. They plow that area away so that apparatus can easily gain access to the road. They are also the ones who do any necessary road work to make driving in and out of the fire station as easy as possible.

Establish a good relationship with the road department director. You'll find that once you show your appreciation for what the road crew does, they'll take every opportunity to help the volunteers when they can and will make your work requests a priority.

The Water and Sewage Department

Any officer knows that his water supply is pretty darn important. And it's tough to fight a large structural fire when your most accessible hydrant has a static pressure of 25 pounds per square inch, or 25psi.

As you and your officers locate specific hydrants with poor pressure, or hydrants with caps that are difficult to open, you are going to need the water department personnel to handle those matters. On an even larger scale, you may identify an entire section of town where the water-main sizes are not adequate for present large-scale firefighting, let alone future fires, if there is further growth and occupancy on existing space.

The head of the water department is one person who can be of tremendous assistance. He can support a plea to the town council that the community's limited water supply system is risky from a fire protection perspective. Like the road department, don't sell these public employees short. They, in their own way, also make for a safer community.

Working with public officials, the media, and the community is a large task that requires hard work and effective planning. Your role as an officer has a lot to do with success or failure in this area of fire department management. The cardinal rule here is never to assume that outside groups or constituencies understand how your department operates or the pressures and limitations under which you work. It's your job to let them know if you want them to work for you.

> *Departments large and small are now, more than ever before, forced to practice fiscal responsibility and careful budgeting. We face proposals that demand reductions in public sector spending. And to compound the problem, it takes more turkey dinners to pay for equipment and apparatus. Our alternative is clear—we must be masters of justification and implementors of sound spending policies.*
> —WILLIAM ANDERSON, ASSISTANT CHIEF,
> GREENSBURG VOLUNTEER
> FIRE DEPARTMENT,
> GREENSBURG, PENNSYLVANIA

4 / Budgeting and Financial Management

Members of an organization can work in public service and maintain a high esprit de corps. But their best organizational goals may go unaccomplished if the supporting financial system fails. An organization is a business, whether it's a corporation, a public agency, a civic group, a fraternity, or a volunteer fire department. And a business needs money to run.

Sound financing is vital to a volunteer fire department. A chief and his officers need money to operate at a level equal to the public safety needs of the community.

Not every volunteer fire chief has the luxury of a guaranteed budget every year. Like a paid chief, the volunteer fire chief competes with other municipal expenses for funds. At the same time, the volunteer chief sometimes has more financial problems than a paid chief. A paid department receives a set amount each year from the municipal or county government. Because taxpayers pay for it. The volunteer chief often must depend on the generosity of citizens to contribute, either through door-to-door canvassing or other fund-raising activities.

This chapter looks at the predominant financing systems volunteers use to support their expenses and operations and presents a successful budgeting model that volunteer chiefs can use.

Volunteer fire departments throughout the United States get financed in a couple of ways. Each has its advantages and disadvantages. Let's take a look at both systems.

The Incorporated Independent Volunteer Fire Department

The term "independent" means two things. First, the fire department is not officially controlled or operated by municipal or town officials. Some operations are coordinated through particular municipal officials. But the independent department is free to establish its own charter, purchase its own equipment, select its own members and officers, design and incorporate its own rules and regulations, and operate on the fireground as its leaders see fit and without interference.

The second meaning of "independent" relates to budgeting, to economic independence. The fire department's officers have the right to spend their revenue as they wish. If they decide that the department needs a new pumper, they don't need permission from the town council or the mayor to develop specifications and solicit bids.

Some municipalities give a set amount of money to their volunteers. This revenue is exclusively to cover expenses in protecting township property. That's all. But there is still no municipal control on how the chief and his volunteers spend any other money they receive. The remainder of operating expenses comes from fund-raising activities.

ADVANTAGES

The independent department has certain advantages. The first is that fire department members are free to govern their own organization. They avoid local interference in a number of ways. One example concerns recruit selection; the independents are not bound by any municipal or county civil service regulations for accepting applicants. And they don't have to worry about any municipal officials influencing who the fire department accepts or doesn't accept for membership.

A second advantage is the freedom to purchase equipment that the chief and members choose. It's up to the president, chief, trustees, and membership to decide when is the appropriate time to replace old engines or trucks with new ones.

Third, the independent department can commit as much of its capital to specific budget items as it wants. No individual or formal body, other than members, can tell the independent fire chief how much from any one line item he can spend on purchases in that category.

DISADVANTAGES

Despite the benefits of operating as an independent operation, members of volunteer independent departments also tolerate some disadvantages in their system. One of the biggest disadvantages is an unstable and tenuous financial structure. Independent fire departments are at the mercy of the community: If residents want to donate, they do; if they don't want to donate, they don't. As the economy is continually rising in a rampant inflationary spiral, homeowners are understandably setting financial priorities. The homeowner who thinks his home is safe from fire thus decides not to donate to the volunteers, or at best to give a minimal contribution. Fund-drive chairmen who project their budgets on an average donation of $15 or $20 from each homeowner are never going to meet their goals if residents decide to give only half that figure or nothing at all.

The situation is not any better with retail and commercial businesses. An independent department chief can only suggest that these businesses give a certain amount. The municipal government—through the mayor, township council or town fathers, and business administrator—sometimes assists the fire chief by appealing to businesses to support the fire department. Nevertheless, it's entirely up to the store manager or his home office to authorize a donation, and sometimes the donation doesn't come close to representing the size of the establishment and what its fair share should be as compared with what the average homeowner gives.

Some of the advantages of an independent system are unfortunately outweighed by this financial disadvantage of not knowing where the bulk of next year's funds are coming from, how much these funds will be, and whether the money will meet all the financial needs of the fire department.

Volunteer Fire Districts

In parts of the country where there are still large concentrations of volunteers, such as in New Jersey and on New York's Long Island, the volunteer fire district is the primary organizational design.

Volunteers in different parts of the country have different definitions of what a fire district is. In Nassau County, New York, for example, a community may have as many as three companies in one department. In that district, all three companies respond to fire calls anywhere in the community. In parts of central New Jersey, though, there are towns that have more than one fire department. But each fire department responds only to fire calls within the geographical boundaries of its district. A department will not respond to a call in one of the other districts, even though all the districts are in the same town, unless there is a call for mutual aid.

Fire districts are increasingly replacing independent departments. Independent volunteers find themselves too vulnerable to the ups and downs of the nation's economy. They cannot accurately predict how willing the community will be to contribute come fund-drive time, and what will be the effect of poor contributions on the fire department's financial stability.

One major difference between an independent department and a department in a fire district is that, under the guidelines of a district, a fire department is guaranteed some revenue for its operating and planning expenses. Residents of the town, township, or village pay a set amount for fire protection in their municipal taxes.

Since fire department revenue is under some direct control

by municipal government, there must be an official governing body of individuals to present the fire department's financial needs to the town and this group is the Board of Fire Commissioners. Fire commissioners run for a seat on the Board and must be elected by a majority of votes in a general election. This is the most effective way to run this system. Through an open election, candidates can publicly promote their qualifications for holding office. The community elects these individuals based on their qualifications and potential to function in an objective, democratic, and effective way.

Advantages

First, in a volunteer fire district there is some definable revenue for operating expenses. This is more financially sound than operating solely from revenue received from fund drives. It also helps fire department leaders set and meet their objectives more realistically than independent volunteers can do, given the limits of available funds.

Second, communities with a moderate to high proportion of industrial and retail businesses (as opposed to strictly residential areas) can reap a high revenue from those businesses. Just by assessing each business a defined amount of money earmarked solely for fire protection expenses, based on the total square footage of the business, a volunteer fire department district has a financial safeguard against a residential taxpayer's revolt and lower revenue from homeowners for fire protection. Part of the philosophy of encouraging business and commercial growth in a community is to ease the tax burden on the town residents while guaranteeing needed revenue for the municipality.

A third advantage of fire districts is that the likeliest candidates for seats on the Board are the volunteers themselves. This doesn't mean a situation where the fox is watching the chicken coop, with the volunteers unethically controlling their finances. But volunteer committee members do understand the system, both its present short-term needs and its future long-range plans. Nevertheless, some volunteers believe that having many firefighters serving as fire commissioners is dangerous. They tell of departments in districts where commissioners budget excessive funding requests for a particular stationhouse at the expense of the others in the department.

A fourth advantage is that guaranteed income for fire protection may mean lower insurance rates for the municipality. The benefit is a reduction in overall costs to the taxpayers. More money can pay for necessary equipment. And communities are looked at by insurance companies to see how well their fire departments are equipped.

DISADVANTAGES

A disadvantage can occur when the Board of Fire Commissioners is represented by a disproportionate number of individuals who know little or nothing about emergency services organizations such as the volunteer fire department. Sometimes the civilian wants to have a voice in the fire department's spending power simply because that revenue comes from public taxes. Aside from that fact, he doesn't care about fire protection in his town. This kind of person may be irresponsible and show little regard for the real purpose of being on the Board. He may not take the time necessary to learn all he should about fire department organization, operations, system planning, or equipment requirements.

Just as some volunteers think that commissioners who are also firefighters present no problem, others do not see civilian commissioners as a disadvantage. In fact, they say that a fire commissioner who is *not* a firefighter may be more objective in evaluating the fire department budget because he is not partial to any one particular engine or truck company in the department.

A second disadvantage to a volunteer department in a district is that it is vulnerable to public opinion about the necessary costs for fire protection services compared with other municipal expenses. For example, the Board of Fire Commissioners may be represented by an equitable mix of firefighters and citizens who understand the emergency services needs of the community. They work for the best interests of the volunteers and the community.

Now the good luck stops. Town officials may reject proposed expenditures for fire protection, no matter how legitimate they are, because they already feel a disproportionate burden from other municipal expenses. If the community is up in arms about high property taxes and a bond issue for school repairs, town officials could reject the commissioners' request for, say, $500,000 toward the purchase of three new engines and one new tower ladder.

Proposition 13 fever is contagious. Even municipalities that have volunteer fire protection services can suffer the wrath of the taxpayers' revolt. It's often tied to the myth that says, "Fire will never strike my house, so I am well protected and don't need to pay any more fire department expenses."

Some fire departments operate within a district under another title than fire: water, library, community service, and others. In California, some volunteer departments are in a designated water district. Some volunteers see this as an advantage for them. Here, the fire department or district has a budget for fire protection, but it can also charge fees to community residents for the cost of water used in fire protection.

In Nassau County, New York, there are also fire departments in water districts. But some volunteers there see the setup as a disadvantage. They complain that the community employs paid commissioners for water district activities and that these commissioners make water issues, not fire protection, their top priority.

Finally, there is the municipally controlled volunteer fire department. But this is usually a semantic difference between the terms municipal and district. The municipal department still has a Board of Fire Commissioners, its expenses come primarily from the community tax base, and its budget is governed ultimately by the town's municipal leaders.

Part Paid/Part Volunteer Departments

The Washington, D.C., metropolitan area has many part paid/part volunteer departments. Fairfax and Prince William counties in Virginia and Montgomery, Prince Georges, Baltimore, and Frederick counties in Maryland all employ career firefighting personnel for fire protection services. Each of those counties has volunteers as well, some with more volunteers than others. In Montgomery County, for instance, 750 paid firefighters and 1,000 volunteers serve a population of 605,000.

ADVANTAGES

Volunteers in a mixed system have a big advantage over volunteers in other systems, for the county or municipal tax revenue that supports the expenses of the paid personnel also helps the volunteers. In the Washington, D.C., area, there are many new and modern stationhouses with fine accommodations for apparatus rooms, dormitories, lounges, kitchens, and meeting and repair areas. These accommodations serve the paid firefighters—but the volunteers also have the use of them.

Many of these mixed departments operate as individual organizations that administer and regulate their own operations. In addition, the fire chief is sometimes a volunteer who oversees at a given fire whether the officer in charge is a paid or volunteer officer. Some mixed departments have the best of all worlds. They can solicit donations from the community because they are called a volunteer fire department and are, for the most part, self-governed. At the same time, they are assured of enough money to maintain and upgrade apparatus, equipment, and physical facilities, courtesy of the taxpayers.

A second advantage to the volunteers in a mixed system is that they usually have access to a training academy that serves the paid firefighters. An excellent training academy is in Rockville, Maryland. The director of Fire and Rescue Services manages it and heads a staff of career and volunteer personnel who provide formal training in every area from EMT training and structural firefighting to hazardous materials and defensive driving.

All volunteer firefighters in Montgomery County are eligible to enroll in these programs. They all comply with NFPA Standard 1001 for firefighter levels I, II, and III levels of certification, as well as for fire officer levels I through IV. Through the county program, volunteers must successfully complete specific levels of training if they want to qualify for certain fireground officer positions in the department.

The bottom line is that the volunteers receive, free of charge, the benefit of excellent training, both in content (because it complies with recognized and accepted standards) and in physical resources. For an independent department in a municipality to build such an academy would be highly unlikely.

DISADVANTAGES

One financial disadvantage of being a volunteer in a part paid/part volunteer system is being vulnerable to the whims of the taxpayer. In California, where Proposition 13 originated, volunteer fire departments have suffered from the taxpayer's purse tightening. Though there are not as many mixed departments in California as there are in the Washington, D.C., area, all fire departments, paid and volunteer alike, have suffered financial setbacks.

All Americans think about the rising costs of goods and services. If they respond by mandating a tighter rein on spending, then municipal or county services are affected. Volunteers in a mixed system are never as vulnerable as independent volunteers, but they are vulnerable nonetheless.

There is one other disadvantage to being a volunteer in a mixed system that is not related to finance but is important enough to discuss. Interpersonal relationships between paid and volunteer firefighters can range from mature mutual respect to all-out warfare. In departments where paid personnel are directed by paid officers who expect the volunteers to perform their job in a professional way, then the likelihood of paid and volunteer firefighters existing in harmony is good. There is hostility between paid and volunteer firefighters when the paid firefighters think of the volunteers as irresponsible, immature, and incapable of handling the responsibility of a tough, dirty, and demanding job.

The volunteers have their biases too. They see the paid firefighter as someone who is more interested in starting union job actions than in protecting the public. To the volunteers, the paid man looks on firefighting as just a job. This friction can manifest itself in many ways. One is in arguments and disagreements as to how fire department money should be spent between the volunteers and their paid counterparts. It's a bad situation, and it usually deteriorates until a crisis is reached.

The Budgeting Process

A budget is a financial statement. It tells a person what it will realistically cost him to fund his objectives. Objectives are the key. A chief must first set them, then arrange them in priority order. After that has been done, he can adjust his delivery of service based on committed funds and priority objectives.

Budget issues affect every volunteer fire chief whether he manages an independent, district, municipal, or part paid/part volunteer department. He has to budget. In this section I present a budgeting design that is effective and compatible with a volunteer fire chief's financial duties.

Zero Based Budgeting

Zero Based Budgeting, or ZBB, has become a popular financing system in recent years. Both the federal government and numerous state governments now use it.

ZBB is a useful resource for the volunteer fire officer. It helps him prepare a budget based on priorities of service;

evaluating performance in terms of allocated funds, and identifying both low- and high-value functions. Because he uses it with priorities and performance in mind, the chief prepares a budget that is more detailed than before, as well as more realistic.

ZBB works well under two conditions. First, it is a good resource when the local officials operate with a ZBB resource allocation system. And second, it must be seen that it takes a minimum period of three years of use to measure the effectiveness of the ZBB system.

ZBB also works well when the volunteer fire chief and the town's business administrator both use it. Then both are familiar with ZBB design and requirements. When both sides sit down to discuss service delivery and funds allocated for those services, each will understand the other. In addition, only in the two years or so after implementing ZBB can a chief see how effective he was in assessing priorities, low- and high-value areas, and the performance levels he met with the money he had.

BENEFITS OF ZERO BASED BUDGETING

ZBB is more practical than other budgeting systems for a number of reasons. First, it is incremental. Instead of a single budget submission, there are actually four budgets, each specifying what services will be delivered and what it will cost.

1. *Minimum:* This is the lowest level that the fire department can operate at and still provide a realistic degree of effective fire protection and prevention. When you plan a budget at the minimum level, your committed resources usually come to about 65 percent of the present budget.
2. *Reduced:* The reduced budget level comes to approximately 80 or 90 percent of your current budget. It's greater than the minimum budget level, so the level of service is greater.
3. *Current:* Next year's budget level is the same amount of funds that you operated with during the present fiscal year. Though you

budget for the same funds, you can make allowances for cost increases that are likely to occur. An example is the inflationary cost of goods and services that come with the purchase of new apparatus that will be delivered in two years.
4. *Improved:* The improved budget surpasses the current budget. When you want money to improve what you currently deliver to the public and to add other services, you show this in the improved budget. This level is usually 110 percent (or more) of the current budget level.

You propose all four budget levels at the same time. This allows your municipal manager to assess the fire department's plans for services and performance and how they are affected by varying funding levels.

A second benefit of using a ZBB system is that the planning and prioritizing comes from the bottom and moves up. In the volunteer fire department, junior or company officers can budget their needs. Then they can submit them to the assistant chief and chief for a review and possible change. The chief then submits them to the local government or fire commissioners.

There is a twofold value in this. First, the junior officers take part in planning, setting priorities, objective setting, and assessing. The chief may choose to modify some of the budget plans and priorities. Yet the junior officers can discuss the issues openly and cooperatively. There is a strong participatory management system that is active when junior officers, chief officers, and bench officers work up the budget. The second value is that the fire department is going to municipal leaders knowing exactly what it needs to maintain current service, what it will cost to do more, and what will be sacrificed if funding is reduced. So often in the passed-down system, municipal leaders give the fire department some funds, and there is no recourse for the volunteers. Why? Because they had no idea what they would do with the funds they received. I'm talking about the difference between saying, *What will we get this year?* and, *This is what we want this year.*

A third benefit of ZBB is that the fire department knows

exactly what it will and will not provide for any given budget that the local government is willing to support. As a result, the fire department is not accountable for services it cannot realistically deliver as a result of insufficient resources to provide those services.

William A. Ward is a management professor at Virginia Polytechnic University and has held numerous public administration positions in federal and state government. Dr. Ward has designed an effective four-phase worksheet for the fire manager who participates in ZBB.

Figure 4.1 illustrates the first phase of Dr. Ward's model: the *minimum level* of funding. All the essential facets of the budget are present: performance narrative, service not provided or excluded, differences between minimum and current levels, and workload changes/known cost increases.

An example is the independent fire department that gets a set amount from the local government and canvasses for the rest. Low allocations from the township and poor contributions from residents may force the independent fire department to reduce its response units as a result of the increasing cost of fuel. A minimum level budget shows this. It may state that the fire department will not be able to answer commercial fire calls with a full assignment of three engines, an elevating platform, and two chiefs, as it would be able to do if there were increased funds for that level of service.

The *reduced level* worksheet, shown in Figure 4.2, is the same as the minimum-level budget worksheet except that the differences are now between the reduced and current levels. The *current level* budget projection shown in Figure 4.3 has some different categories. First, the fire chief must explain major program goals, performance/program evaluation measures, and workload changes/known cost increases. These are important factors because the current level for next year's budget is the same as the present one except that it adds inflationary costs. As a result, local leaders want to know how fire protection/prevention services will change or improve from the past for the same amount of money. The *improved level*

MINIMUM LEVEL	ORGANIZATION:	PROGRAM:
MANAGER:	Percent of Current Level _____	RANK _____	TOTALS: $$ _____ positions _____

PERFORMANCE NARRATIVE: (Describe Services & Objectives)

SERVICE NOT PROVIDED OR EXCLUDED:

DIFFERENCES BETWEEN MINIMUM AND CURRENT LEVELS:

WORKLOAD CHANGES / KNOWN COST INCREASES:

COST BREAKDOWN:		SPECIAL NOTE:
$$$$$$$	positions	items

Figure 4.1 ZBB Four-Phase Worksheet: Minimum Level.
Reprinted with permission, International Association of Fire Chiefs, 1980.

part of the model shows all improvements in fire and rescue emergency services that could be made if money were not a limiting factor. Figure 4.4 shows where the fire chief discusses improved services and the differences between current and improved levels.

Notice that the performance narrative for each budget level requires the writer to describe services and objectives. This provides specific detail on just what services will be offered based on allotted funds.

The ZBB Process

Zero Based Budgeting should be used with simple, clear, and short budget forms. By "short," I mean that summaries should not exceed two pages. The ZBB process should be a practical approach, not one bogged down by numerous stipulations that make it as difficult as the federal budget. The same goes for the way you prepare and deliver it. Use only the paperwork necessary to prepare your budget.

After they write their summaries, the chief and his officers are ready to list, by priority, the objectives they expect to accomplish. This priority list affects what service delivery levels they project for a specific budget level.

For example, the chief may decide that EMS (Emergency Medical Services) has a higher priority than having fire prevention tasks conducted under a reduced budget. If this is so, he shows that decision in his budget and level of service. When he reaches a reduced funding-level projection, he can probably omit low priorities entirely.

Discussions between a chief and his officers are called *ranking*. The ranking of objectives of priorities in terms of budget allocations is done at several levels of the organizational structure. The larger the structure, the more levels there may be. In a paid department of 200 personnel with 14 stations, for example, the company officer may do the first ranking. The assistant chief may review it. And the chief makes final deci-

REDUCED LEVEL	ORGANIZATION:		PROGRAM:	
MANAGER:	Percent of Current Level _____	RANK _____	TOTALS: $$ _____ positions _____	

PERFORMANCE NARRATIVE: (Describe Services & Objectives)

SERVICE NOT PROVIDED OR EXCLUDED:

DIFFERENCES BETWEEN REDUCED AND CURRENT LEVELS:

WORKLOAD CHANGES / KNOWN COST INCREASES:

COST BREAKDOWN:		SPECIAL NOTE:
$$$$$$$	positions	items

Figure 4.2 ZBB Four-Phase Worksheet: Reduced Level.
Reprinted with permission, International Association of Fire Chiefs, 1980.

CURRENT LEVEL	ORGANIZATION:	PROGRAM:
MANAGER:	Percent of Current Level _____ RANK ____	TOTALS: $$ _____ positions _____

PERFORMANCE NARRATIVE: (Describe Services & Objectives)

EXPLAIN MAJOR PROGRAM GOALS:

EXPLAIN PERFORMANCE/PROGRAM EVALUATION MEASURES:

WORKLOAD CHANGES / KNOWN COST INCREASES:

COST BREAKDOWN:		SPECIAL NOTE:
$$$$$$$	positions	items

Figure 4.3 ZBB Four-Phase Worksheet: Current Level.
Reprinted with permission, International Association of Fire Chiefs, 1980.

IMPROVED LEVEL	ORGANIZATION:	PROGRAM:
MANAGER:	Percent of Current Level _____ RANK ____	TOTALS: $$ _____ positions _____

PERFORMANCE NARRATIVE: (Describe Services & Objectives)

EXPLAIN IMPROVED SERVICE PROVIDED:

DIFFERENCES BETWEEN CURRENT AND IMPROVED LEVELS:

WORKLOAD CHANGES / KNOWN COST INCREASES:

COST BREAKDOWN:		SPECIAL NOTE:
$$$$$$$	positions	items

Figure 4.4 ZBB Four-Phase Worksheet: Improved Level.
Reprinted with permission, International Association of Fire Chiefs, 1980.

sions from the final decision on ranking priorities. He may agree or disagree with the rankings of his company officers. Though he needs the input and recommendations, the final financial report to local officials contains his ranking of the most to the least important priorities at the four budget levels.

Next, local officials review the chief's report. Business administrators, city managers, and finance directors then decide (1) whether they concur with the objectives for fire protection services and (2) which budget level the fire department will receive.

For a volunteer fire chief, the ZBB process is slightly easier than it is for a paid chief. There are two reasons for this. First, there are not as many bureaucratic layers above a volunteer fire chief, and that means not too many people can change his plan. There really isn't anyone else above a volunteer fire chief except a mayor or township business administrator and the town council. This differs slightly in a fire protection district; there, the chief's budget must go through the Board of Fire Commissioners before it is presented to local leaders for approval in the overall municipal budget.

In addition, the volunteer fire chief commands no paid personnel unless he is in a district with either paid dispatchers or paid drivers. Since there is no capital expenditure for salaries, which usually account for 95 percent of budget expenses, he can budget his money for other line items: equipment (maintenance and repair and purchase), supplies, contingency or emergency funds, and capital improvements (stations).

The initial part of ZBB is the collective problem solving, decision making, disagreement, and resolution between the chief and his line officers. In the volunteer department this process is usually limited to about ten people. I'm talking about budgeting for fire protection services. The group's size may expand if the president and fire chief budget collectively for firefighting and administrative expenses.

This approach differs for the independent fire department. Because the independent department chooses not to be under local control, only firefighting expenses are reflected in the budget levels for township donated funds. The chief can be assertive and fight for what he needs in terms of fire protection services. But it's unreasonable to ask the township to finance administrative, nonfirefighting expenses such as tables and chairs for a meeting room. In this instance, the president of the fire department should develop administrative funding levels, based on ZBB, that will be financed by community funds and not township-donated funds.

Once this problem-solving, participatory management process takes place between the administrative and operations officers of the fire department, all volunteer department leaders must be consistent in their budget projections. They should agree that if local leaders change the fire department's list of priorities, the department will hold fast to what it can and cannot deliver for a particular funding level. It's important to present a unified front based on realistic priorities and objective setting, instead of a dart-throwing approach of *we'll take what we get and then decide how to use it*. The first approach comes from a strong assertive base; the second, from a submissive one.

An important part of ZBB is to specify levels of service delivery that are innovative and more effective in terms of public protection. It's one thing to have an improved budget level that includes purchasing a new 1250-gallon-per-minute pumper, merely to have a new engine. It's something else, and much more sensible, to have an improved budget level through which to finance the training and equipment needed to provide basic life-support EMS delivery to the community.

Fire departments, paid and volunteer, are no longer immune to public cutbacks and financial restraint simply because they provide emergency services. Proposition 13 is living testimony to that idea. Because they are fixed-base operations, fire departments need to explore new and effective services that are also cost effective over the long term. Purchasing that new engine might make a negligible difference in services. Firefighter-EMTs might, over time, reduce the mortality and morbidity rate in the community by a significant degree.

The volunteer fire department is a business, and it must operate that way. An essential part of any business is a sound financial operation. Zero Based Budgeting is an effective method for a chief to use as he plans service delivery with limited financial resources. It's an assertive approach for the volunteers, and it's one they should use more often in the future.

The ability to make accurate judgments rapidly under emergency fireground conditions is essential in an effective officer. And one thing is certain—when he is on the fireground he is in charge and he is responsible. Company and senior officer fireground leadership is so vital that no chance should be taken on any but the best.

—WILLIAM PECK, EX-CHIEF,
EAST BRUNSWICK INDEPENDENT
FIRE COMPANY,
EAST BRUNSWICK, NEW JERSEY

5 / Fireground Officer Selection

Ideally, every line officer should be elected to office based on these valid factors: a demonstrated understanding of fire-suppression skills, tactics, and operations; a demonstrated ability to behave maturely, constantly showing poise, self-control (particularly on the fireground), responsibility, and open-mindedness; strong interpersonal relations with his firefighters; a solid performance record in training attendance; a strong performance record in fire department activities and functions; and general behavior becoming an officer of the fire department.

We know that this is not always the case. If, for example, two volunteers are on the ballot to become lieutenants at a company station, it is conceivable that the less qualified candidate will be elected simply because he is more popular. And that can be a poor reason. The more popular candidate may spend a lot of time at the bar downstairs on weekends. Or he may help repair some of the members' automobiles because he is a good mechanic. He is popular, but this has little to do with his ability to command firefighters effectively and handle fireground operations in the midst of noise, confusion, smoke, imminent disaster, darkness, and inclement weather. Because we are not perfect, our emotions and biased feelings sometimes cloud our judgment.

Volunteer firefighters are gregarious, people-oriented individuals. They enjoy one another's company. A quiet, introverted person is sometimes poorly suited to the volunteer fire department. This is a place where getting along with others is important. Members let themselves be the butt of humorous kidding and the focal point of attention, and as easily give it. This camaraderie exists to a far stronger measure than it does in civic and social clubs because volunteers consider themselves very special people. In their minds the essential service they provide is not a responsibility that every community resident would willingly assume.

Some of the same ideas hold true in their relationships with one another. A volunteer who is likable makes many friends. Other volunteers feel comfortable with him and easily build a bond of respect and trust that carries over to the fireground when firefighters work together.

This chapter discusses the selection of fireground officers. You may be wondering what friendship has to do with it. Surprisingly, quite a bit. In some cases, maybe too much.

Each of us has the capacity to respond to things around us in two ways: objectively and subjectively. For instance, we may be standing next to someone on a street corner, waiting to cross. We notice that this person's winter coat is much too small. Objectively, we can tell that the coat is too small because the sleeves end well above the wrists and the front of the coat cannot be buttoned. But we also make an emotional, subjective judgment. How can anyone wear a coat like that and not be embarrassed to appear in public? Anyone who dresses like that has no concern for his appearance. This psychological response is a negative one, and in many cases, you readily make value judgments.

It is important to be liked as a person. Someone who is rude and arrogant may have all the essentials of a good fire officer except one: He cannot relate to people. This handicap will hurt him as a leader if, in fact, he ever becomes one. On the other hand, the awesome responsibility of being a fireground officer is built on so much more than a good personality. Popularity is fine, but when there is an emergency and when people's lives hang in the balance, what it takes to be a good officer is the ability to lead and make decisions instantaneously, in the midst of crisis.

I believe it is possible to select fireground officers who are both well liked and qualified to serve. It takes the effort, though, of all members to select the best personnel.

Modifying the Fire Department Constitutional Process

The general practice in electing line officers is to set aside a date for nominations. After the special meeting in which nominations for office are made, a period of time goes by while all members consider the names on the ballot. That old game of politics appears. Some nominees try to mend personal differences that have existed with others. It's all part of the process, and we accept it for what it is, like it or not.

If there is really an interest to select qualified officers, though, then the place to start is with the bylaws. It is here that valid standards can be set for qualifying as a line officer. Personality is part of it, yes; but it's not all of it.

Officer Selection Board

A line officer selection board should be set up. The board should consist of a formal body of members who are impartial on the line officer selections. No one, anywhere, can be totally impartial. Even former fire chiefs who are still active and answer alarms realize that they will have to take orders from those finally chosen. But some people can be more objective than others. Among the more likely to be objective are ex-chiefs, trustees, members of the Board of Fire Commissioners, and some rank-and-file members. Ex-chiefs are recommended for their experience as fireground officers. Trustees and fire commissioners are recommended because they hold important roles, symbolic of responsibility and capability. Rank-and-file firefighters are the direct subordinates of their officers, and so they should be board members who are highly respected by their fellow firefighters.

Appointment to a line officer selection board should be by majority vote of the membership. Six representatives can conduct a well-rounded, impartial review and assessment of the volunteers nominated for office. One setup, for example, may include two ex-chiefs, two trustees or fire commissioners, and two rank-and-file members. This is only a suggestion; each department must decide on the number and kinds of representatives it wants.

Criteria for Fireground Officer Selection

After their election to office, the officer selection board members must begin the large task ahead of them. It is their job to review and assess how each line officer nominee measures up to standards. Let's assume for the moment that this election year is the first one in which your department is using a line officer selection board. What are the standards for assessment to be?

THE PERSONNEL RECORD

One item, discussed more fully in Chapter 7 on recruitment, is the need for keeping personnel files on every member in the department. The files should contain facts and information on formal training courses completed, letters of commendation from officers and/or citizens, percentage of response to alarms over the years, involvement in fire company projects and committees, and possible statements of reprimand or discipline for past actions or events.

This is a good starting point from which to assess officer capability. A good firefighter shows a consistency in performance over the years. I don't mean that a marginal firefighter cannot turn around and become a model member. Officer selection is a competition, however, and the best candidate should have an impressive personnel record.

Written Examination

One way to find out how much someone knows about a particular subject is through a written test. The nominee who is less than the life of the party may know as much or more about all phases of fire department operations than any other nominee.

Test questions will have to vary. Specifically, questions emphasizing company officer size-up and initial orders as first due on the scene should be the focus on the lieutenant and captain examinations. As we move up the ranks into the deputy, assistant, and chief of department levels, questions should center more on fireground coordination of multiple units, both from their respective companies and from mutual-aid calls on multiple alarms. The emphasis here is on large-scale fireground control and coordination of many men and pieces of apparatus.

Questions for these exams can be of many types: essay, fill in the blank, true/false, and multiple choice. The answers provided should not contain any ambiguous answers. If choices are the form, they should be respectable, logical choices, forcing the test taker to think and to concentrate. Test content is up to the selection board. I have mentioned specific questions for company officers as opposed to chief officers. Other examples of questions:

- Knowledge of standard operating procedures
- Skill knowledge—ladders, overhaul, forcible entry, ventilation, etc.
- Knowledge of fire apparatus—centrifugal pumps, hydraulic systems on ladder trucks and elevating platforms, etc.
- Knowledge of hydraulics principles and practices
- Knowledge of self-contained breathing apparatus

Some may feel that a written examination is not necessary or even foolish. I expect that their arguments against a written test may be just as foolish.

When tests are given, the selection board also has to decide whether to establish a passing score or just let the point total be considered along with other assessment factors. There are merits in both decisions. By setting a particular score as the minimum for passing, the selection board is implying that an officer must have a good depth of knowledge to pass. A score of 75 percent or less would not demonstrate that depth and may justifiably eliminate a candidate. Yet a nominee who gets an average score on a written exam but makes high marks on the remaining assessment categories still may merit a chance. For all we know, he may be the best candidate.

It's really a discretionary call on the part of the board. Either way, it must choose what is fair to the nominees and the department.

THE ORAL EXAMINATION

The written examination score is just one measure of an individual's potential as an officer. A good way to learn more about a nominee's qualifications is through an oral examination.

There are specific reasons for making an oral exam part of the selection process. First, you can ask questions to which an individual must respond right away. Unlike the written exam, where the person can skip a difficult question and return to it later, a question presented orally can help the board evaluate the candidate's ability to "think on his feet."

For instance, a board member may say to the candidate, "You have just arrived as officer of the first-due unit at a working department store fire. What would be your first set of decisions and subsequent actions?" As the candidate responds to the question, the board member can complicate the hypothetical situation with difficult yet realistic questions.

> *Candidate*: My first actions would be to lay a line in from the nearest hydrant; notify incoming units that this

is a working fire; find out if there are any people still inside the building; determine the origin and present spread of the fire; order second-due units above the fire floor to check for fire extension and prepare to ventilate the building, while hand lines are being advanced inside the structure if possible.

Questioner: Upon arrival at the scene, you are told that there may be as many as thirty people trapped on the fire floor. Would you make any different decisions at this point?

Candidate: Based on this information, I would also relay orders over the air for all incoming units to be aware of the life hazard. Also, I would have communication dispatch a minimum of ten ambulances and mobile intensive-care units, above and beyond the usual number of such units normally assigned on this kind of call. Finally, I would have communication contact a minimum of three neighboring hospitals to have their emergency personnel send nurses and doctors to the scene to set up TRIAGE [victim injury assessment] as well as be prepared for the arrival of patients suffering from smoke inhalation and burns.

Questioner: It's not until you are at the scene that you remember the large water-main break that occurred the day before. Your static pressure off the hydrant you laid in from is only twenty-five psi. Yet your fire structure is almost three stories high and one hundred seventy-five feet wide. What are your problems now?

You can see the point of this questioning. It throws roadblocks in front of the candidate. But the limiting situations are meant to be realistic and definitely possible. The speed with which the candidate answers is the same quickness he's going to need to react at the fire scene, except that there he has to cope with noise, smoke, and heat.

Another use for the oral examination is to find out the candidate's responses to issues that are just as important as a fire scene command. Here are two examples:

One of your firefighters is trying to qualify as a driver and pump operator, but to date he has not passed all the necessary requirements. He is allowed to drive only when you are present, and not to fires. One day when you stop at the firehouse on the way home from work, you learn that this individual drove the apparatus to a fire that morning and almost caused a major traffic accident. How would you handle this situation?

In recent weeks you have witnessed a growing personality clash between two of the volunteers at your station. You are not certain what factor or factors brought about this conflict. But you do know that it exists and is getting worse. It has now reached the point where both of them are having differences while at a fire, in the presence of civilian bystanders, and it's interfering with fireground orders operations. Furthermore, both have threatened to quit. You don't want that to happen as both volunteers are good firefighters and respected by the other members. Yet their differences are causing serious problems. What actions would you take, and why?

Another advantage of the oral examination is that each candidate has a chance to qualify his responses. Some people do not express themselves clearly in writing. No matter how hard they try, they cannot put into words what they wish to say. The oral exam fairly balances this kind of situation. The candidate can respond to a question in as many words as he feels necessary to justify his answer.

A third advantage of the oral phase is that selection board members can get a stronger feeling of how much confidence or lack of it there is in the candidate's answers. Fireground officers must be decisive, firm in their actions. A candidate who reveals a high degree of uncertainty risks having the same problem at a fire. He may not want to give certain orders despite their absolute necessity. A written exam cannot express feelings of commitment or indecision.

This doesn't mean that because someone is indecisive, he should automatically be dropped from consideration, or that this person should be told he is not officer "material," now or in the future. At the present time, though, his uncertainty about decisions will hold him back from being as good an officer as he could be. In time, and with more experience in the department, he will probably reduce this liability to a significant degree.

One premise of this text is that measuring someone's capability at a particular task should be performance based. The one area where we diverge from this philosophy is in this factor of the oral examination for fire officers.

I haven't stated how the candidate is evaluated by the board in both objective and measurable ways. In truth, he isn't. The candidate's responses are measured subjectively. One board member may feel that the candidate's verbal response to the hypothetical situation is exactly the way *he* would respond. Another board member may have different feelings and thus evaluate the candidate based on *his* personal viewpoint.

Despite the fact that the oral exam is subjective, it is still a very useful tool in the overall assessment process. It's valuable to listen to an individual's response on a question and how that response indicates discriminating reasoning, deductive reasoning, acceptance of responsibility, good judgment, and so forth. One way to reduce the subjectivity of this part of the selection process is to list specific categories and judge the answers to the questions against those categories. Examples are self-control, judgment, oral expression, maturity, self-discipline, reasoning, and confidence.

Assign numerical values on which each response is graded. For example, the highest score a candidate may receive is a maximum of 5 points for each of the specific categories of any one response. Whoever designs this system also has to provide some statement to assist the reviewer in understanding what constitutes a score of 3 or a score of 5. This information, in turn, is transferred to an official rating sheet which can be filled out by each reviewer. Figure 5.1 shows what a rating sheet can look like.

You'll notice that the rating sheet shows both a total score and an average score on each question and response. There is a specific reason for each score. The selection board may decide, with the membership's approval, that the candidate for any given office who has the highest total scores on the oral exam-

CANDIDATE: John Smith

REVIEWER: _____

DATE: _____

Response Question	Reasoning	Self-Control	Judgment	Maturity	Knowledge	Confidence	Total Score	Average Score
#1	3	3	4	3	5		18	3.6

REMARKS:

Question	Reasoning	Self-Control	Judgment	Maturity	Knowledge	Confidence	Total Score	Average Score
#2	4	4	4	4	4		20	4.0

REMARKS:

POINT DEFINITIONS:

1 = Candidate shows no proficiency in the category.
2 = Candidate shows a low degree of proficiency in the category.
3 = Candidate shows a moderate degree of proficiency in the category.
4 = Candidate shows an above average degree of proficiency in the category.
5 = Candidate shows a high degree of proficiency in the category.

Figure 5.1 Oral Examination Rating Sheet, Fireground Officer Selection

ination is the top candidate for that part of the selection process. As for the average score, the board may look at average scores for all oral questions and responses. A demonstrated consistency of high averages may be interpreted as a greater overall capability of the candidate. Two candidates, for instance, could have the same final point totals for three responses. But one may have stronger, or higher, averages than his opponent.

Who is the better candidate? Again, as I suggested with the written test score, this has to be a matter of judgment by both the selection board and the membership as to how they interpret scores.

Fireground Command Simulation

There's nothing like the real thing. People can commit huge amounts of preparation to some event, learn all they possibly can, and be confident that they have considered every conceivable occurrence. But each event is a new experience unto itself.

That goes double for a new fireground officer. People study to be doctors, lawyers, politicians, and actors. There is a sense of genuine excitement when the moment actually comes to perform surgery, prosecute, defend in a major criminal case, speak before the House of Representatives, or appear in front of a large audience. Yet there is something different about individuals who command the actions of people and things at an emergency scene, and firefighters are probably the most visible people there.

The job is tougher than for those other occupations. Those people have time to contemplate, plan and implement their actions. The fireground officer doesn't have this luxury. He must mentally calculate what he hears and sees, combine his calculations with the skill and training he has had, and make immediate and wise decisions.

The selection board, with the approval and cooperation of

the membership, can take this process through one more step. It can find out how the candidate performs at an actual fire. Carried out under closely supervised conditions, a simulation reveals a lot about the candidate. It sounds as though we are talking apples and oranges, but we're not. True, *simulation* means creating a situation that approximates real conditions. But we are also discussing how the candidate commands at a real fire, an unsimulated situation. The point, then, is a compromise: Have the real thing with some controls built in. How is it done?

In some volunteer departments, it is already a regulation that an adult firefighter has the discretion to accept command of his unit if a line officer does not respond to the station and assume his usual responsibilities. When a rank-and-file volunteer makes the decision to sit in the officer's seat, he assumes all the seriousness of the job—it's far more than stepping on the siren and talking over the radio.

Let's take this process one step further. When the selection board is reviewing candidates, each candidate should be allowed to be the officer in charge at a real fire, with all responsibilities, except that the present line officer is there with him all the time. The candidate makes all the decisions, while someone qualified and experienced observes and evaluates all that is happening.

There will likely be some logistical problems to work out in this officer evaluation system, but it can be done with some planning. Nominees for company officer—lieutenant and captain—can be in charge under the supervision of any of the department's line officers. Chief officer candidates should command under the supervision of an officer at least one level higher, preferably two. If the captain himself is nominated for a chief's office, he should be working closely with either the assistant chief or chief during this exercise.

Since a chief usually responds in his own car, the candidate reports directly to him at the fire scene. If it's a working fire, the chief gets a firsthand look at how this individual handles decisions and actions. What you have to be ready for is who will take over the candidate's responsibilities at a fire if he himself is a regular officer. As long as you plan for all this, the system can work.

Notice that I haven't mentioned the selection board in the fireground command simulation. Rank-and-file members cannot evaluate officer skills at a fire scene if they have never been officers. Also, former chiefs and trustees are not always active in answering alarms, and those who were officers in the past may not be as acutely aware of the finer points of effective fireground command as they once were.

The solution is to have the present line officers who are evaluating candidates fill out an evaluation report on the candidate for a minimum of three reviews and submit the report to the board. The board, in turn, will review these findings along with the other selection criteria. A minimum of three evaluations is absolutely necessary, especially for candidates who have never held a line office. When someone knows he is being closely watched, natural tenseness and apprehension can easily interfere with behavior and actions. So you should give each candidate at least three to five simulated command situations to help break that initial tension to the point where he can better concentrate on the fire and demonstrate his highest level of capability and decision making.

Once again, we are confronted with an evaluation system that is relatively subjective. There will never be any *one* correct or "right" way to command a fireground operation. Each situation is different and has its set of unique problems. But specific criteria reduce the subjectivity of the evaluation in simulation.

The most important part of the simulation performance rating sheet is the information written on it. What is the line officer who is reviewing looking for? The following list suggests possible criteria to list on the sheet:

- What conditions existed at the fire scene upon arrival of the candidate as the officer in charge?
- What were his initial orders?

- How did those orders correspond to the situation at the scene?
- Did any situations develop that required a change in tactics, and if so, how did the candidate react?
- Were all firefighters certain of what their orders were?
- How did the candidate coordinate the actions of other units at the fire scene; specifically, placement of other arriving engines and trucks and their manpower?
- What actions and decisions by the candidate would you rate as very strong?
- What actions or decisions by the candidate would you rate as lacking or needing improvement?

Also, the rating sheet for fireground simulation should have written answers to the above questions by the observing line officer. To apply the information of what happened to a numerical form is neither informative enough for the selection board nor fair to the candidate. True, different people will read the rating in different ways. At the same time, so many actions take place, so many decisions are made at a fire scene by an officer, that to rate him with a number, grade, or statement in twenty-five words or less defeats the purpose of the evaluation. Officers who are observers for candidates should write detailed statements and take as much space as they need to say what needs to be said.

One important point when using evaluation criteria is that they are equally applicable to the selection of volunteer EMS officers. Both volunteer and paid fire/EMS providers serve Montgomery County, Maryland, with the largest percentage being volunteer. Many of the volunteers are certified EMTs, and some are paramedics certified according to standards of the state.

It is not unusual to go into a fire station in Montgomery County that has both volunteers and paramedics and find that the ambulance/medic unit officer is a volunteer. For that matter, one of the largest, best-equipped, and professional emergency medical care units in the Washington, D.C., area, which provides both basic and advanced life support, is the

Bethesda–Chevy Chase Rescue Squad in Montgomery County. All the members of the squad are volunteers.

Oral examination questions, written examination questions, and fireground simulation can all be used for EMS officer selection. The only change is that testing is designed for EMS. The selection board can easily develop a series of questions that will measure decision making and judgment by a paramedic during a moment of intense crisis, such as an accident scene, as part of the oral examination phase. The same kind of emotional control that a good suppression officer displays on the fireground is also necessary for EMTs and paramedics trying to revive a victim in cardiac arrest while clearly communicating with and understanding the emergency physician directing them over the air from the hospital.

Standards for Selection: NFPA Fire Officer Qualifications

In Chapter 9 I refer to the National Fire Protection Association Professional Qualification Standards as a basis for fire department training skills. One of those NFPA standards is *NFPA No. 1021: Fire Officer Professional Qualifications*. I want to discuss it in detail here because of its relevance in this chapter.

When the National Professional Qualifications Board of the Joint Council of National Fire Service Organizations finally established "1021" in 1976, it made the following statement:

The intent of this committee [fire service professional development committee for fire officer qualifications] was to develop performance standards in a clear and concise manner so that they can be used to determine without doubt that any person so measured does truly possess the skills to be a fire officer. The Committee contends that these performance objectives can be used by any fire department in any city, town, or private organization throughout the North American continent.

The key to this statement is the emphasis on performance-based objectives. Whenever possible, volunteer fire departments should base their fireground officer selection on valid standards.

Standard 1021 has six levels of fire officer qualifications. Each level adds another set of requirements that complements the related responsibilities as one rises from company officer to chief officer. With the exception of some particular areas of expertise, most relate to volunteer fire officer duties.

Fire Officer I covers the following knowledge: leadership, community relations, fire prevention, fire suppression, fire protection, fire hazards and causes, building construction, codes and ordinances, firefighting strategy and tactics, chemistry, safety practices, fire investigation, and report writing.

In Fire Officer II, the areas of psychology, human relations and management, English, technical math, hazardous materials, and technical report writing are added. You can see the blend of technical understanding with the ability to write and communicate.

Fire Officer III covers fire protection systems and alarm systems, water supply systems analysis and fire protection hydraulics, fire protection administration, English, general physics, public speaking, personnel management, sociology, major emergency planning, and public relations.

Fire Officer IV moves on to safety practices, industrial fire protection, organization and management, public finance-budgeting, fire suppression and detection systems, and public relations. (You'll notice that some categories apply more to paid officers.)

Fire Officer V covers political science, public administration, state and local government, national government, and legal aspects of fire protection.

Finally, Fire Officer VI, the highest level, sets competency standards in master planning, management information systems, labor relations, and public administration.

Why Recognize "1021"?

A volunteer fire chief interested in higher standards for selecting fireground officers is only one voice. Everyone else in the department may be satisfied with the way line officers have been selected in the past. Why change? You may be one of these chiefs, willing to fight the battle but still out on a limb by yourself. You would like every member of the department to be as encouraged about applying "1021" standards to line officer selection as you are. That means educating them.

The first advantage you can praise about "1021" is that its standards, from Fire Officer I through Fire Officer VI, demand a well-rounded degree of knowledge and skill. A good officer has to know more than just fire suppression and water supply systems. He must speak and interact with the general public and local officials as a member of fire department management. That's why public speaking, public relations, and public administration are important subjects. He must also serve as a leader of people, and so personnel management and human relations are necessary.

A second value of "1021" is that practically all the identified categories are useful to a volunteer fire officer. With the exception of labor relations, each level of "1021" adds another set of professional skills for becoming a more effective officer.

A third advantage is that "1021" is designed to stress areas of knowledge that become more important as one moves from company to chief officer. Because an assistant chief or chief of department meets with more public officials, subjects such as master planning, state and local government, and public administration are as important as are fire hazards and causes.

A final reason to promote "1021" to membership is simply that it's there. The National Fire Protection Association has designed a practical set of standards for officer selection. No volunteer organization to date has done as much. Why reinvent the wheel?

Returning the Results to Membership

After all candidates have been tested, the selection board returns to the membership with the scores, grades, and reviews of all line officer nominees. At this point, the selection board has completed its job. It should not and cannot have the right to recommend which candidates are best qualified to be fireground officers. That is up to a majority vote of the membership. If the membership is committed to a formalized selection process, they will really use the board's results to decide who will be the next group of line officers for the department.

Selection by Standards: To What Purpose?

I have discussed a number of methods for selecting qualified, capable volunteer fire officers. Chiefs of department, company officers, and any other volunteers who read this book may decide, either individually or collectively, that any or all methods are desirable to use, both now and in the future.

There is another message in all of this. Fireground officers should be selected on capability, not sociability. When a homeowner needs the volunteer fire department, he or she does not care whether the officer who arrives on the engine is popular, spends a lot of time in the social room, or can put up paneling in the standby room. What the public does care about and expect is that the officer is a highly capable firefighter, knowledgeable about his duties as a fireground officer, and able to make sound and accurate decisions quickly and with confidence—and that he can efficiently coordinate and direct his subordinates during an emergency situation. The public has every right to expect all of that.

A major step forward for the volunteer fire service is to upgrade its professional standing by selecting qualified line officers. In order to do that, it must use valid, measurable standards. Let's put the past tradition of electing officers as though it were a personality contest just where it belongs: in the past.

> *Morale and motivation are married by necessity. If either is not used in a positive manner, then a breakdown in the organization is imminent.*
> —THOMAS M. HAWKINS, JR., FORMER CHIEF
> VIENNA VOLUNTEER
> FIRE DEPARTMENT,
> VIENNA, VIRGINIA

6 / Morale and Motivation: Managing the Volunteer

Many books have been written on the subject of personnel management. People study for degrees in industrial relations, industrial psychology, and human resources management, all for the purpose of learning how to manage other people. Conferences and symposiums are run all over the country each year, just to let people meet and discuss new and changing trends in this field.

This chapter does not go into a long dialogue on all the facets of personnel management. Instead, my purpose is twofold: (1) to analyze the situations and opportunities where a volunteer officer can improve his abilities at being a more effective manager of people, and (2) to discuss the kinds of personalities that can help or hinder you as you manage firefighters.

When a fire officer issues orders on the fireground, he can be pretty much assured that his orders will be carried out without argument. The fire department is a paramilitary organization and must operate this way. In moments of crisis, firefighters don't have time to analyze the merits of any given decision. Unlike a group of businessmen meeting to discuss adding another piece of machinery to a production line, fire officers and firefighters cannot casually sit down and discuss whether an interior attack should be made in a burning building. An officer must decide for himself, based on his experience in past situations, his technical knowledge, and the conditions of a fire at any given moment.

There is another side to all of this. The degree to which firefighters have confidence in an officer's decisions is a measure of the respect they have for him as a leader, a manager. He doesn't earn this respect only at the fire scene. It also comes from his ability as an officer to motivate and inspire his firefighters—individually and collectively, on the fireground and off. I'm talking about managing people, one of the toughest, most challenging tasks there is.

Every volunteer firefighter faces some rough going the first time he becomes a fireground commander. It's ironic that the newest fire officer, the company officer, has little leadership experience yet has the toughest job. He is the first one at the scene. He has to make the initial decisions that will prove to be wise or unwise.

Just as important is the fact that this new officer will be around his troops more than the fire chief will. When there are disagreements to settle, the company officer is the first mediator. When his firefighters don't want to go out on a rainy Monday night training, he is the one who must motivate them. When a firefighter decides to rebel against authority, it is the company officer who has all eyes on him, seeing how he chooses to face the situation. When an irate citizen comes to the firehouse with a complaint, it is he who must set the example, be the model for his men, in dealing with the situation. How interesting that those with the most to learn as officers are the ones most often on the firing line.

These young officers inevitably look for an example to follow, for someone who has the experience and talent necessary to bridge the gaps of human differences that exist so that goals get accomplished. That person may be you, a chief officer.

You are the model for all your firefighters, officers and rank and file alike. Your responsibility for many jobs is overshadowed by a fundamental one: managing people. Studying leadership styles is worthless if you cannot be sensitive to people's needs, desires, interests, problems, abilities, and feelings. The example you set for your firefighters can serve as well for your present and future officers. The ability you demonstrate as a manager of people can be copied by those who watch and serve under you. So can your weaknesses. It should come as no surprise, then, that this is probably the toughest job for any officer.

Some may argue that learning how to motivate and inspire people is not as simple as I just described it. Maybe they're right. But we sometimes fail at a task because we assume it's too complex right from the beginning. It's like a pump operator being absolutely puzzled because he isn't getting water through the lines. He has a water supply, the pump is engaged, the throttle is up, there is positive pressure registering on the main discharge gauge, and all the hand-line nozzles are opened. But, no water. He assumes that the impeller has malfunctioned. Actually he has overlooked the simplest solution: opening up the discharge gate.

The lesson we can learn from this is that managing people does not have to be a difficult job. Oftentimes, the solution to personnel problems is as simple as the common sense necessary to see it. And that's the approach I'm going to follow.

Working through the Chain of Command

An organization operates through a functional, formalized system or hierarchy. Members of the organization clearly understand who they are responsible to in the organization as well as their own status.

How easy it is to assume that because there is a recognized system, everything naturally works out as expected. Not so. In reality, the formal system in an organization is as weak or as strong as the people who run it. The system operates successfully when people follow its rules. Order can become chaos when people do as they please.

These ideas are important in a fire department. Throughout

history and continuing today, the fire department operates under a paramilitary system. Every firefighter must clearly understand the individual and collective responsibilities of everyone in the department. The chain of command is the established system in the department. How the chief operates under it affects the morale and motivation of his volunteers. We realize why the chain of command operates as it does on the fireground. But away from the fire scene is another matter.

The chief who requires that all members of the department comply with the chain of command should serve as an example himself. There are a couple of reasons for this. First, each company officer is the ranking authority at his station. As such, he has full responsibility for handling any and all matters that come up as the first link in the management chain. Because of this responsibility, he deserves the *earned* respect of his company members in deference to his position.

Let's say that a township resident comes to you, a chief or a company officer, about one of your firefighters. He states that he has seen this volunteer drive his car at high speeds while responding to the fire station. And in an area where a lot of children play. The resident is worried that someday this volunteer may injure a child with his reckless driving habits. What is your reaction to this situation?

If you are a chief officer, you should immediately discuss the matter with your company officer from that station. He must be the first officer to talk this matter over with the volunteer in question. For you to step right in and take matters into your own hands will cause two subsequent problems: (1) you will have damaged the company officer's status in the eyes of his men because your taking charge of the matter gives the impression that you don't trust the company officer to handle it properly, and (2) you will have alienated and embarrassed the company officer. Why should he show any further respect for you? Aren't you telling him to honor a chain of command that you yourself have broken?

It's a different story if the company officer speaks to the volunteer about his driving habits, but to no avail. It may reach an assistant chief, and by that time the thought of dismissing the volunteer from the department is a legitimate alternative. At least you showed respect for your company officer by allowing him to take initial charge of the problem. You showed respect for the system and for the company officer's rank. In return, you earned respect. Company officers and volunteers quickly learned that you are concerned about them as people and that there is a way to work with and through the chain of command to run a good fire department.

A second reason for honoring the chain of command is that you can devote your time and effort to matters that really warrant attention. A volunteer chief who tells his officers that he expects them to honor the system but interferes in every matter that comes up, regardless of how trivial it is, is essentially defeating the purpose of the system. If he intervenes in everything that comes up, then he won't have enough time for the really important matters. That's why the system is in place, so that problems you handle go to you, if you are chief, and problems at a lower level of command go to a junior officer.

The Open-Door Policy

The chain of command is important, but you should be flexible when you use it. You must adapt to situations that must be handled in special ways. Essentially, maintaining an open-door policy is a way of letting your firefighters know that you are approachable, that you are around to discuss problems with them. It is an excellent alternative to working with people when the regular channel of communication, the chain of command, is inappropriate.

People's personalities inevitably conflict at one time or another. With the best of intentions, a company officer may have trouble relating to his men. They are following his orders, but they don't respect him as an officer. One of the volunteers has been having particular problems with this officer. He feels that the officer has unfairly singled him out for criticism. This situation really disturbs him, and rightly so. What's he supposed to do with the problem? He doesn't want to sit down and discuss it with the company officer because the atmosphere is already hostile.

This volunteer needs to know that a chief is there to listen and help him reach some resolution, to defuse a potential time bomb. The chief *should* be there. The morale of his personnel is important. The company officer is reluctant to say anything about the situation, expecting that it will settle itself. Maybe, maybe not. If the chief's door is not open, then he might find out about the problem only after things have gone too far.

You should realize that an open-door policy has responsibilities that go along with it. The first is being a good listener. Listening is an often neglected skill in human communication. Very often, as we listen to what others are saying, our minds are rapidly absorbing the information as we form value judgments about what we have heard. In fact, we really weren't listening to what the other person was saying, or even what the person was not saying through expressions and physical gestures. The skill of listening is most effective when the listener is truly trying to find out what the other person is saying *and* feeling.

Good listening means clarifying things. Restating what the person has said in your own words shows that you've been listening. This makes the speaker feel more confident that you really do care about his problems. If you have misinterpreted something your firefighter said, then restating it or asking for clarification guarantees that what you are hearing and understanding is exactly what the person is trying to say.

A third part of being a good listener is to refrain from passing immediate judgment or rendering an opinion based on what you would do. Instead, learn all you can about the problem by asking the person questions. This gives you information, and it may help the other person discover possible solutions to his problem.

For example, you think that one alternative for the strained relationship between a company officer and a firefighter is for the two of them to sit down and state how they feel, to talk candidly and get things out in the open. Knowing how the volunteer feels at this point, though, your suggesting such a course of action may turn him right off. He'll think to himself, "Why did I bother to come to a chief officer? He's telling me to go talk to the very person I don't want to talk to. This was really a waste of time." By using listening skills, your approach is to say to the volunteer, "This is a serious problem, and I would like to see it resolved before it gets any worse. I'm sure you would, too. How do you think that can be done?"

The result is that the volunteer himself may suggest that he speak to the officer and get everything off his chest. He's not happy about the idea—but it was his idea, and not yours. And it's more acceptable to him than if you had suggested it yourself. You accomplished the same end result, and your volunteer walks away appreciating that you cared enough to listen. Once again, it earns you respect.

Hearing the Whole Story

As a chief officer, you have the final word on most matters. The consequences of final judgments rest with you. Keeping this in mind, you can begin to see how essential it is that you make decisions based on a full knowledge of all the facts. This is really important when you manage people. You are the judge in personnel matters that come up.

For example, one of your officers may come to you and insist that he wants to put one of his men on disciplinary suspension, pending a hearing, for overtly disobeying orders at a fire. These are serious charges that cannot be taken lightly. Since you decide whether or not to discipline the volunteer (if so stated in your bylaws), you must get all the facts. Up to this time, you've heard only your officer's version of the story. What about the volunteer in question? Shouldn't you talk with him for a serious charge like insubordination?

I think you'll see that discretion and good judgment are needed here. Having a talk with the firefighter is absolutely necessary. He may not know what his company officer is thinking, and it's also possible that he did *not* disobey orders. His officer's words could have been drowned out by some other noise, such as a siren, engine roar, or radio transmission. Or this could be a veteran firefighter who has always been dependable, someone you wouldn't expect to disobey a direct order.

Imagine your embarrassment if you suspend the volunteer based solely on your conversation with your officer. When the volunteer counters the charges with convincing arguments, you lose respect. You failed to extend the common courtesy of letting the volunteer answer the charges before placing him on the spot in front of his peers. It's unlikely that the members of the department will feel that there is any due process in the fire department.

The consequences of such actions can hurt morale. Other volunteers may assume that the same thing can happen to them, and it is sure to have an effect on the way they feel. Because morale and motivation are so important, remember that managing people works when there is fairness and equity for all. The fairer you are, the more your volunteers will respect you.

Giving Effective Feedback

All of us tend to take feedback for granted. We expect it. Whether it comes from friends, relatives, peers, or supervisors, we generally realize that it will tell us something good and something bad. But we pay more attention to feedback from others when it's frequently weighted on the negative side, or when it doesn't come at all when we expect it to.

Feedback is important to everyone. And it's very important to any leader that he offer feedback—especially a leader such as a volunteer fire chief. Because volunteers give of their time without compensation, they need to know that someone thinks they're doing a good job. Words of support and encouragement can help build dedication, hard work, and pride.

It's a far more difficult job leading a volunteer fire department than a paid one. A volunteer chief doesn't always have an assured budget every year. He doesn't get a certain amount of money every two or three years to hire new recruits. He can force his firefighters to comply with the rules and regulations only so far; they don't depend on being firefighters for their livelihood. For these reasons, a chief must use timely and effective feedback to maintain morale and motivation.

Specialists in interpersonal communication and influence say that the first part of any feedback affects how the person getting it behaves. You gain more from honey than vinegar, as they say.

Let's say, for instance, that an officer is having a tough time with some of the volunteers. He doesn't have their respect. As his senior officer, you have observed him and have seen that one of his biggest handicaps is that he continually gives negative feedback; he seldom says anything good. The volunteers have come to expect this negative behavior from him. They find it hard to show respect for someone who doesn't believe that respect is mutual.

Now you have to intervene. You know that taking this officer aside and criticizing him will earn you the same negative respect that he gets from his men. You're acting just as he does. You can accomplish so much more by beginning the conversation by telling him what he's doing well and why you feel that way. You're showing that you're willing to recognize his good accomplishments. When you get around to the subject areas in which he needs to improve, he'll be mentally and emotionally prepared to take some constructive criticism.

Feedback is useful only when it is specific. That goes for both positive and negative feedback. When a superior tells us that he's pleased with our work, we need to know just what it is we're doing well. When we get specifics, we now know what we're doing well and can continue to do it well.

If you're giving negative feedback, be sure to be specific. Take the case of the officer who is not relating to his men. Think how useless your criticism is if you simply say to him, "I don't think you're relating very well to the volunteers, and they don't seem to respect you. I think you'd better straighten out the problem right away." Maybe you have identified a problem, but you haven't done anything to remedy the situation. How can you expect him to change his behavior if you don't give specific instances when his behavior caused problems? Your feedback is helpful only when you cite particular instances where the behavior, had it been different, would not have alienated the volunteers.

Your feedback is useful only when it relates to some behavior that the person can change. To imply that volunteers don't respect their officer because he has a speech problem or wears glasses is absurd. He cannot change those things. It's a different story if you tell your officer that he's losing control because he judges his men before he learns all the facts. Your criticism at least gives him the information that he must work on getting all the facts before making a decision. Patience and control in making decisions is behavior that one can improve.

These same principles hold true for groups as well as individuals. After a rough fire, you may be thinking about some tactical mistakes that were made. To hit on these first in a group meeting makes little impact. Take the time to praise your members for what they did well at the fire. Show them that you both appreciate and respect their efforts. They will be much more prepared to accept their errors. And when they choose to listen, they're less likely to make the same mistakes again.

Feedback works when people listen to each other, whether they are praising or criticizing, and when they give the other person a chance to talk. Common sense dictates that giving negative feedback is useful when the other person has a chance to answer back. If you tell that officer of yours that he's too quick to judge his men, give him the chance to respond, to state why he feels this is happening, and collectively you can make plans to solve the problem.

You may find this information so simple that you think it doesn't even need mentioning. Yet we fail to realize how often we violate these fundamental principles of human communication. If there's a problem, it must be the other person. I communicated clearly! Maybe clearly, but not effectively.

Showing You Care

Showing concern for the other person, showing that "you care," has a strong effect on morale and motivation. A social scientist may state some ten to fifteen rules to follow for effective communication and understanding to take place between people. As a volunteer officer you may speak with one of your junior officers tomorrow and violate practically every one of those fifteen rules. But your talk may go well because your expressions, your tone of voice, and your mannerism expressed that "you care."

If one communicative skill or behavior can do more than any other to build motivation, caring is that skill. You should work at showing that you care constantly. Talk with close, personal friends and get feedback from them about whether you show this concern when talking with others. If you do, continue to do it. If not, start developing a caring attitude.

When you have line officer meetings, discuss this caring skill with your senior and junior officers. Promote an "I care" attitude as one of the most valuable skills an officer can use in maintaining strong morale.

Awards and Incentives

Our society values awards as symbols of recognition and accomplishment. The ultimate in athletics is the Olympic gold medal, and on the battlefield it's the Congressional Medal of Honor.

Awards in the fire service are usually given for an act of heroism and valor, and this is understandable. There are certainly acts of heroism in the volunteer service. But the fact that volunteers serve in communities that are not as densely populated as the urban area reduces the number of major fires and, along with that, the number of rescues.

Because a volunteer has a slim chance of being honored for a heroic act, the department should have other awards and incentives that are just as important. It's all good and fine that volunteers are proud of the job they do. Yet each of us, at some time or another, needs to be recognized publicly. The greatest honor is to be recognized by our peers for what we've done well.

The volunteer chief has a lot of influence here. He can suggest awards, and the membership will probably listen to him. If there is an idea for a new award in the department, the chief is an excellent person to sponsor it. Putting aside for a moment the emotionalism attached to awards, every chief must carefully consider some necessary ground rules before he presents his ideas to membership.

All members must have an equal chance to compete. Any fire department award will strengthen morale if all members have an equal chance to earn it. The department that gives an award to the volunteer who answers the highest number of alarms for the year violates this rule. Sure, the department is fortunate to have some members who answer 85 percent or better of all calls throughout the year. The problem is that some firefighters have their own businesses in town and can take the time to leave their jobs and answer a fire call. Everyone does not have an equal chance to get the award. The winner feels great, but the others resent it. What started out as an award has become almost a punishment for others.

Awards should be based on performance, not personality. People like to compete for awards if they know they are based on valid performance standards. There is nothing necessarily wrong with an award for Firefighter of the Year as long as the standards for assessing and selecting a winner are both equal to all and based on measurable performance.

Let's say, for instance, that a given volunteer fire department has a Firefighter of the Year award. Prior to making the award official, a committee was organized to identify the specific standards for the award. They were:

1. Attendance percentage at mandatory training and at house and apparatus maintenance

2. Participation in fire company committees
3. Extra projects and responsibilities completed (based on the fact that all members had equal opportunity to commit the same amount of personal time)
4. Performance on the fireground, based on evaluation from line officers for the following standards:
   a. knowledge of firefighting skills
   b. carrying out orders properly and with expedience

It's difficult to remove *all* subjectivity when evaluating someone's performance. But it is possible to list objective standards, as the ones listed above try to be, standards that are fair and equitable to all. Only in this way can an award help morale and motivation, not destroy it.

Awards must be in recognition of significant contributions. A department starts with one or two awards. Then the idea begins to "snowball" and eventually ends up with a minimum of six or seven awards. Some believe that the more awards you give out and the more members you honor, the more morale goes up. The problem with this philosophy is that the awards are indiscriminate and no longer represent something special. So many awards are given out to make people feel good that important awards lose their significance.

You can't please everyone. Limit yourself to promoting the most important awards of the fire department, and only those awards. Abiding by this suggestion prevents what started out as a good idea—to promote morale—from deteriorating into the mass distribution of meaningless awards.

A chief can influence what awards, if any, are given by the department. But it is also up to the membership to decide whether they wish to have an awards system and what awards they select. Here are some suggestions for awards that you might consider sponsoring:

1. *Firefighter of the Year:* recognizing outstanding service to the fire department from a variety of valid standards: firefighting, contributions to the department, community service

2. *Valor Award:* awarded when a volunteer attempts or effects a rescue at great peril to his personal safety
3. *Letter of Commendation:* placed in the volunteer's personnel file as a reference to an outstanding action or contribution to the company, either on or off the fireground

Again, these are only suggestions for awards. But they're awards that comply with the previously stated ground rules.

Support Your Firefighters

I've often heard the expression, "You can strip a person of all his possessions, but you can't strip him of his self-respect." Unfortunately, life's realities sometimes contradict this expression. Some leaders have a flair for reprimanding and even humiliating their subordinates in public, a practice commonly called "going for the jugular." I cannot think of anything that does more to destroy self-esteem than this practice. This kind of behavior is about the worst a leader can display.

You can use this tactic in two ways. The first is the way you speak with subordinates in front of the civilian public. The other is the way you speak with them in front of the fire department "public."

Firefighters are going to make mistakes on the fireground; actions are fast and emotions are high. Sometimes the mistakes are serious enough so that a firefighter gets injured. An example is when we warn firefighters who are on the inside of a structural attack not to leave the building without letting their partner or an officer know.

You might have a situation like this while you're in command. You may want to reprimand the firefighter right there on the spot. Your better judgment should win out. It's bad enough that if you lose control of yourself, your firefighters will witness your yelling. More serious is that members of the public will also witness it.

The public expects you and your personnel to know your job. Sure, they understand that all people err from time to time.

Nevertheless, they don't expect it of you. Furthermore, they should not know when you do make a judgment error unless it is a grossly negligent action that may cause an unnecessary injury or death. As volunteers, you and your firefighters must work twice as hard as career men to prove your worth, unfair as that may sound.

I'm not telling you to back down from reprimanding a subordinate when the action calls for it. But be wise enough to do it in private; keep it a matter for you, the firefighter, and his company officer. Behind closed doors you can rant and rave, if that's your style (I hope it isn't). At least you haven't humiliated the subordinate in public. As well, your image as a responsible leader doesn't earn any points if you decide to lay down the law in full view of everyone. You can do without that kind of publicity.

How you handle mistakes and their subsequent discipline affects morale. When you reproach someone, choose carefully where and how you do it. Discipline through good sense, not emotion.

"What You Say Here, What You Hear Here, What You See Here, Stays Here"

Organizations with high morale usually have one common trait: Only the members know and deal with problems. The public doesn't know about them.

This is an attitude that you, as an officer, should insist on and cultivate. Fire department members should feel assured that they can discuss any issues, that they can even argue, freely and openly, without worrying that outsiders will find out about them. When your department's problems become the talk of the community, it doesn't do any good for morale.

For that matter, you should be tough on firefighters who are discussing confidential fire department matters with people who have no reason to know about them. Any member who violates this rule should have organizational sanctions brought against him. Motivation certainly suffers when poor leadership and other problems are not resolved. Nevertheless, hold firm to the belief that no member under your command "wash fire company linen in public." Don't let a bad situation become worse.

Morale and motivation are fundamental to organization stability and effectiveness. They should be as important a part of your management plan as leadership and fireground command. Individuals perform well when they are motivated to do so. Esprit de corps is a valuable commodity. Don't take it for granted, and let good sense and sound judgment dictate your behavior.

> *One important dimension of a good volunteer fire department is the quality of its members; mature, intelligent, motivated, level headed, and highly capable. And we have to seek these people out. Any volunteer organization can gather warm bodies. Quality and not quantity, though, must be the fundamental requirement for the most dangerous occupation in the world.*
> —WILLIAM GOLDFEDER, LIEUTENANT, MANHASSET-LAKEVILLE FIRE DEPARTMENT NO. 3, GREAT NECK, NEW YORK

7 / Recruitment

Americans are joiners. They join and serve organizations like the American Red Cross, Rotary International, Elks, Boy and Girl Scouts of America, 4-H, and others. Most of these organizations serve social or community service interests.

Some 2 million people throughout the United States have chosen the fire departments in their town as the one organization they most like to belong to as a member. This attraction to the fire service is part of an American tradition going all the way back to Ben Franklin's first fire department in the United States, the Union Fire Company, organized on December 7, 1736, in Philadelphia.[1]

What motivates someone to be a volunteer firefighter? Why would he risk possible injury or death when he could be in a "safer" organization? Knowing that firefighting is one of the most hazardous occupations in our society, why wouldn't a person be content to give his free time to the community recreation advisory board of the Knights of Columbus?

We always hear about young boys who dream of becoming firemen or policemen. And most people get excited when they're walking along the street and hear and see approaching fire engines, with sirens screaming and light flashing. It's a unique feeling. Thousands go to and from work each day, doing a job that seems routine and uneventful. The attraction of other interests that break the monotony and, in the case of firefighting, add that special dimension of a dangerous but exciting job is really stimulating. For these and other reasons, firefighting is a job that will always attract people, especially to the volunteer system. It offers a chance to be challenged and tested.

Knowing these things, who would be a model applicant to recruit? What kinds of volunteer firefighters would you like to have in your department, and what personalities would they have? What should be your recruiting standards? Here are some considerations:

1. *Stability and dependability.* Your best firefighters turn out to be those who are dependable, those who know their job and do it right, on the fireground and off. They have stable tempers and personalities not prone to irrationality. They take orders easily and without argument, and carry them out without an officer constantly having to check up on them.
2. *Physical condition.* Firefighting is a grueling, strenuous job that demands a high degree of physical ability. An effective firefighter has high levels of muscular strength, muscular endurance, and aerobic fitness, and low levels of body fat. Poor physical health is a risk to the firefighter and all those around him.
3. *Employment record consistency.* An applicant who has a consistent work record will usually be just as consistent as a firefighter. Rather than be here today and gone tomorrow, this individual will be committed to the fire department. You will be able to depend on him to make a real contribution to the department and the community.
4. *Maturity.* A model applicant to the volunteer service comes recommended by his past and present employers as well as his neighbors and friends. He relates well with most people, and his personality lets him easily adapt to the stressful, tension-filled environment of firefighting. He can deal with criticism and discriminates between appropriate and inappropriate times to confront controversial situations or issues with others.
5. *Prior experience.* The model applicant has some prior firefighting experience combined with a positive evaluation and recommenda-

tion from his former chief and officers. He can ease into your fire operations system without too severe a change in his life style.
6. *Public service work.* Ideally, an applicant has some previous experience in community projects. He is usually willing to serve others without expecting any compensation aside from the satisfaction of doing a good job. This frame of mind toward public service is desirable in an applicant.

No human being is perfect. We all adapt and react differently to the world around us. Because we all have unique and imperfect personalities, an "ideal" applicant is not going to walk into your firehouse. Each applicant will possess both strengths and weaknesses when matched against your model. Since some men will certainly have more pluses than minuses, you must evaluate both abilities and liabilities. Here are some ways to go about it.

Planning Your Recruitment Program

To select applicants, you need applicants. You have to let the community know that your department wants new blood. In Chapter 3 I discussed a variety of means you can use to inform the community of the job you do. As an officer, encourage the membership committee to use these opportunities to the fullest. At any open house sponsored by the fire department, there should be someone available to discuss membership duties and responsibilities to any interested person. Have applications as well as membership qualifications and requirements information available for anyone to fill out right there or take home with him.

Give prospective applicants your name and phone number so that they can contact you if they have any further questions about the fire department and how it operates. Potential members who want to discuss membership will approach you with a degree of respect for the office you hold.

The Membership Committee

A good membership committee convenes on a regular basis to discuss the strengths and weaknesses of the recruiting system. Because they have established goals and standards—for example, goals for the number of new members they would like to have in one year's time and the standards for selecting those people—their chances of success are much stronger than those of a committee that operates with no direction or purpose.

You have the opportunity to play a major role in shaping the committee's direction. I mentioned earlier that the caliber of your men reflects directly on you as an officer and on your department. The questions you should be asking committee members are these:

- What members are doing the preliminary screening of applications? Are they in this position with my approval and recommendation as such to membership?
- Who serves on the interview committee for the fire department? Are the line, bench, and rank and file represented to my satisfaction? Should I meet with them, prior to their interviews, to find out how they plan to handle the session?
- What kinds of things are being discussed in the interviews? Are the committee members doing all the talking, or does the applicant have a chance to express his own thoughts, thus enabling the committee members to better assess the applicant's future role in the department?

We are all too familiar with the name of an applicant coming up for majority vote of the membership as a probationary firefighter. The interview committee spokesman tells membership, "We have met John Smith and he seems like an OK kind of guy. We recommend that he be accepted for a six-month probationary period." Maybe the committee members did all the talking during the interview and left without really learning anything about the applicant or letting him speak for himself. Their only "impression" is that this person is an "OK guy."

The Membership Application

A good application will tell you a lot of important things about your applicant. You should promote this phase of the recruitment process. But don't be surprised if you come up against some stiff opposition by certain members as you try to institute a better application form. Their attitude will be that the fire department neither has the right to be nor should it be that soul-searching in its application process. Well, if your accepted duty is the protection of life and property from fire, then there are times of stress in a fire when there isn't a second chance to do the job right. The more you know about your applicant, the better you can judge his future worth as a firefighter.

You should continually review the application used by your department. Does it tell what you really want to know about the applicant? Are there particular sections of the present application that can be omitted and other sections that need more detail? What should be added that gives more information on the applicant and lets you make a better judgment?

After you have reviewed the application and have written down your thoughts on any possible changes, set up a meeting with the fire department president, the membership committee chairman, and the trustees or Board of Fire Commissioners. You need these individuals on your side when you bring the new application before membership for a vote. Do your homework. Deliver a strong case for changing your application, and you will find that you have support when membership discusses the issue on the meeting floor.

To get to this point, you have to come up with a justified rationale for the new application. Different organizations ask for different information on their application forms. There are, however, certain details that are germane to you and the rest of the department. A model application might contain this information:

Part 1: General Data

This is the general information usually listed on all applications: name, address, date of birth, marital status, name of spouse if married, person to contact in an emergency, criminal record, driving record, and so on. Be careful to check which questions or inquiries in this section an applicant is not required to answer, such as questions that come under the Federal Privacy Act, which prevents discrimination on the basis of sex, age, race, creed, or ethnic origin. Your state and county civil service commission can advise you on this matter. A mistake here can leave you open for a civil suit at some future date.

Part 2: Employment History

What the applicant does for a living is not as important to the fire department as how long he has been doing it and his record of employment. I'll cite two examples to highlight this point.

Applicant A is twenty-seven years old, lives in his own apartment and works during the day packing boxes in a large publishing company's shipping department. He wrote on his application that he has worked at this particular job for four years. He's used an average amount of sick time in those years.

Applicant B is also twenty-seven years old. He wrote on his application that he is at present unemployed but that he recently worked as a store manager with a grocery chain. In fact, he has worked at five store manager jobs in the past five years. He also has his own apartment.

What's your first impression of these two applicants after reading their employment histories? Would you say that Applicant B is a better choice as a firefighter because he has held a number of jobs as a store manager and therefore shows potential as a leader? What about Applicant A? Is he not as good as Applicant B because he packs boxes for a living? From your standpoint as a fire officer, you might see Applicant A as the better choice from the employment perspective. Why? Because the fact that he packs boxes is immaterial. What is important is that he has been doing that job for a long time. He has demonstrated his dependability, whereas Applicant B has gone from job to job.

The fire department needs volunteers who can be counted on to make a personal investment in the department's future and not join only to leave four or five months later. A person's employment history shows some important things. If you feel that Applicant B, for example, is also a good choice, then insist that the membership committee talk with his past employers to get a complete idea of the kind of worker he is. And see to it that you or your membership committee chairman interviews Applicant A's boss, too, either on the phone or in person.

One final thought. Get the applicant's written permission or a waiver to check into his employment history. This usually allows the applicant's references as well as his former and present employers to be less inhibited about what they say to you or other members of the fire department. And have the waiver notarized.

Part 3: Applicant's Written Portion

Volunteer firefighters will tell that it's not unusual to want to be a volunteer and yet never once be asked by an interviewer *why* you want to be a firefighter. This brings us back to the kind of person you want to recruit for the volunteer fire service.

The application form needs space for the applicant to write something about why he wants to be a member of your fire department. Even if nine out of ten applicants say something unbelievable like "to serve my fellow man with distinction and honor," you at least gave them a chance to express their feelings. What they write may surprise you, and at the same time, it may pinpoint an undesirable attitude. Again, don't assume that every applicant thinks as a "model" applicant.

Part 4: Nonfire Responsibilities

One section of the application should list all the various committees of the fire department, such as grounds, house maintenance, fund drive, meeting room rentals, county fair, county firefighters' association, membership, apparatus and equipment purchase, and others. The applicant should have a space to check off some of the department functions on which he wants to work. Granted, he may not check off anything, indicating that his only interest is in the firefighting end of the operation. This doesn't necessarily mean that this person will not be a good firefighter. But volunteer organizations demand some extra effort on everyone's part to make them successful. An applicant who is anxious to work on department committees may turn out to have that extra edge over other applicants. He is willing to do what is required as a firefighter, and more.

You might want to approach membership on opening the ranks to applicants who want to serve strictly in a nonfirefighting role. This is unusual in a volunteer fire department. After all, fighting the fire is the real excitement of the job. But there are people who want to help their fire department without necessarily riding on the engine or truck. Their assistance is something worth thinking and talking about with your officers, trustees, and general membership.

Part 5: Prior Experience in Firefighting

You may believe that requesting information on previous firefighting experience needs no explanation of its value. The answer is both no and yes. You obviously want to know if any of your applicants have been volunteers in other departments. If they have been, they will need less training in firefighting skills than someone who doesn't know a hydrant gate from a hose clamp. That's obvious and doesn't need any explanation. All you will need do is to orient an experienced person to those particular fireground evolutions practiced by your department.

But asking about previous experience doesn't necessarily mean not needing any explanation. You might have an experienced volunteer from a neighboring township or community move into your district and file an application for membership. Your reaction should be: What kind of firefighter was this person while he served in his former department? Did he do only what was asked of him and no more, or did he contribute to the success of his department? Was he considered dependable and reliable, a good firefighter, by his officers and peers? Were there ever any incidents in his past record when he behaved in a way unbecoming a firefighter, let alone a public servant?

This last question is particularly important. None of us is perfect. Each of us has, at some point in our careers, made technical errors and used less than good judgment at the fire scene. If we haven't tried to attach a supply line from another engine to our discharge gate instead of our intake, then we've stood at the pump panel as the driver watched the attack line lie limp and uncharged while the throttle is winding out at 2500 RPMs, only to discover that we forgot to engage the pump when we stepped out of the cab. All firefighters, paid and volunteer, make mistakes at some point in their firefighting experience.

As the chief, it's your job to contact the chief from your applicant's former department. He might tell you unequivocally that your applicant was a well-respected member and had he not had to move out of his former town, may well have been a line officer in a few years. On the other hand, he may be quite vague when you contact him. He may hesitate or refuse to say anything beyond the bare fact that "John Smith served as a member of this department for two years." That says something in itself. A response like this should prompt you to probe some more. This kind of answer from a former chief of an applicant sometimes indicates that he was more than happy to get rid of your applicant. He is implying that there were some serious problems with your applicant.

For example, the other chief might have suspected (possibly not provable, but suspicious nonetheless) that your applicant was choosing his fires—not getting out of bed on a cold January night for a washdown at 12:45 a.m. yet responding for an odor of smoke in a warehouse 45 minutes later on another call. If your regulations require that your men respond to everything unless they are (1) on sick leave, (2) out of town, or (3) watching their infant children, then you don't want this person in your department, regardless of his previous experience as a firefighter. Again, I return to the belief that you don't have to accept just any applicant. You want people you can depend on; you want people who are responsible all the time, not part of the time. Because you manage an all-volunteer force, you can't afford to settle for "I didn't feel like making the last fire, Captain."

Health and Fitness

Research has shown that firefighting is one of the most hazardous occupations in the United States; it exceeds construction, quarry mining, and law enforcement.[2] At the same time, heart attacks and other forms of vascular disease account for almost one-half of all firefighter deaths in the line of duty.[3] These figures are generally quoted when referring to the paid fire service. That should be absolutely no reason to disregard health and fitness figures as irrelevant in the volunteer service. Floor collapses, backdrafts, and heart attacks don't strike only the career firefighter.

Just as the chance of a major conflagration happening in your town is always present, so is the chance of you or one of your men suffering a disabling injury, especially a heart-related injury at a fire. Fire departments across the country are starting physical fitness programs to increase the level of cardiovascular fitness along with the level of physical capability needed to fight a fire.

A successful physical fitness program has many factors: effective planning, sound management design, understanding how fitness is important to a firefighter, motivating individuals to stay fit, establishing standards for fitness achievement, reducing the risk factors contributing to cardiovascular disease as it affects firefighters, legal liabilities, and others. Ideally, you should have a mandatory physical fitness program for your new recruits right away. But even a voluntary program is better than no program at all. It is certainly understandable when an all-volunteer department starts a program strictly on a voluntary basis. After all, the men don't spend their working hours at the stationhouse as do the paid firefighters. Nevertheless, it can be done in a volunteer department, both for veterans and new recruits.

An excellent case is the Greensburg, Pennsylvania, Volunteer Fire Department. This all-volunteer department has a highly successful fitness program. Many members participate in the program and are highly motivated. It began with every firefighter who ran 100 miles receiving a "100-mile club" T-shirt. Interest was so strong to continue beyond that point that participants are now eligible to earn a warmup jacket, a warmup suit, and a hooded sweatshirt for progressive distances. All the clothing has been designed especially for the Greensburg Fire Department. These clothing awards have proven to be great incentives, and Greensburg volunteers work hard to earn them.

Medical-Physical Assessment

Every applicant should be required to go through some form of official medical clearance before being accepted into the department. Some chiefs may feel that this is being too tough in an all-volunteer department. On the contrary, an individual may fight fires and, unbeknown to either you or him, may be suffering from some serious heart abnormalities that could cripple him under even a moderate degree of physical strain and exertion. If a heart attack strikes him on the fireground, everyone is going to suffer—the man himself, his family, the town that has to cover his medical expenses, and you the officer. You stand to suffer because you have lost the services of a good member and fine firefighter and because you may have left yourself open to a legal suit should someone question whether the firefighter should have been doing the work in the first place.

The questions, then, are these: How do you find out if an applicant is physically able to perform strenuous firefighting tasks when called on to do so? How do you find out if an applicant is taking a risk because of his state of health? What health-risk factors are associated with firefighting? What criteria should you use to distinguish the physically fit applicant from the unfit one?

Let's first discuss the cardinal factors contributing to cardiovascular disease, the number-one killer of firefighters in the line of duty.

1. *Elevated blood pressure.* Hypertension is a health problem for the entire population. It is critically important in firefighting. Firefighters continually operate from periods of relaxation and sedentary life styles to immediate response at a fire alarm. High blood pressure results in damage to the arterial walls of the vascular system, and the effect on the body can be severe when combined with other risk factors.
2. *Elevated blood cholesterol.* Medical evidence has shown that high degrees of serum cholesterol, caused by diets high in saturated animal fats (i.e., red meat, dairy products) are directly responsible for speeding up the atherosclerotic process, commonly known as hardening of the arteries. It is this buildup of fatty lipids and plaque that adheres to vessel walls and restricts blood flow both in and from the heart.
3. *Smoking.* Aside from being a cause of cancer, smoking poisons muscle tissue. Carbon monoxide has a greater affinity for hemoglobin in the blood than does oxygen, and it therefore deprives the muscle cells of necessary oxygen. Sufficient oxygen is crucial in firefighting. Professionals in medicine also believe that nicotine causes damage to the inner arterial walls and increases the destructive process.
4. *Obesity.* Your total body weight is comprised of two factors—lean body mass (muscle tissue, bone, and organs) and fat tissue. Physiologically, males with a level of fat weight in excess of 20 percent of their total body weight are bordering obesity and taxing their

hearts. Fat weight in excessive levels can kill a firefighter, just as can high blood pressure.
5. *Lack of exercise*. Being out of shape prevents the heart from meeting the excessive demands on the human system. Firefighters, above all other occupational groups, need to be physically fit through proper cardiovascular conditioning and exercise, with emphasis on muscular strength and muscular endurance of the upper body.

What value is this information to you as an officer? To begin with, you can spot dangerous levels of some of these risk factors in your applicants before they become members. Granted, you cannot demand that an applicant stop smoking, but you legitimately have every reason to find him unfit for membership because he is a physical risk—to himself, his fellow firefighters, and the public.

Enlist the services of a competent physician in your town to serve as the fire department doctor. He should be (1) a cardiologist, (2) a sports medicine-oriented doctor, and (3) a doctor who understands the physical demands required in firefighting. For a reasonable fee, a physiologist can measure some of these critical risk factors. The fire department should be willing to pay to have all final applicants undergo a 12-lead resting electrocardiogram to check for any potential heart problems. Serious heart problems often don't show up unless the individual undergoes a stress-tolerance test on a treadmill monitored by a trained professional. This is a very costly procedure, and not every volunteer department budget can handle it. At the least, your physician can make a preliminary evaluation of the applicant's condition from the resting EKG, medical history, and a physical examination.

Paul O. Davis and Howell Wright, exercise physiologists and health and fitness consultants to fire departments across the country, have designed a useful recruit selection process design that appraises the health (among other measures) of a fire department applicant.[4] Though their system is designed primarily for use by a paid department, a number of phases of the system are useful to the volunteer department. They suggest an initial health appraisal consisting of (1) blood pressure; (2) vision; (3) color vision; (4) resting EKG; and (5) body composition, or percent of body fat. Trained fire department personnel can make these evaluations. Beyond that, health measurements such as blood chemistry to measure cholesterol levels, glucose, and the like, and a 12-lead resting EKG are not that expensive as health predictors. Performing these tests could save the department and the town a fortune in future disability payments. Both your fire department physician and a reputable medical laboratory can administer these tests.

The decision whether or not to require a physical fitness exam prior to accepting an applicant varies from department to department. It is unlikely that many all-volunteer departments require applicants to pass a fitness exam before they become firefighters. Maybe the time has come for the volunteer service to take a major step forward. Is it enough to know that your applicant is a mature individual and demonstrates strong potential as a member and firefighter? Is it enough to know that your applicant's health is within acceptable limits? Whoever said that volunteer firefighters should *not* be tested for a level of physical fitness that indicates the capacity to perform firefighting skills?

Aerobic fitness, or the body's ability to use oxygen maximally during work, and high degrees of muscular strength and muscular endurance are critical physiological factors in firefighting. Davis and Wright have researched the need for a fire department physical fitness test that is not only a valid test but one that can accurately predict firefighting ability.[5] A test instituted by your department should meet these requirements. Otherwise, an applicant who fails your physical test may have grounds for a legal suit. He may believe that your test did not measure what it should have.

The National Fire Protection Association's Standard 1001, Firefighter Professional Qualifications, specifies minimum physical fitness requirements for firefighters. The test battery assesses some of the essential physical fitness components, such as aerobic fitness, muscular endurance, and muscular strength of the upper body. Some exercise physiologists working on fitness measurement and assessment for the fire service have questioned the "1001" standards. The issues in question are (1) who designed the test battery, (2) the person's or persons' qualifications in the field of physical performance assessment in firefighting, and (3) the fact that the test battery has not been validated.

I don't want to cast aspersions on the National Fire Protection Association. The volunteer fire service is increasingly adopting the "1001" standards in qualifying volunteers on the Firefighter I, II, and III levels. For this reason alone, any fire chiefs using these fitness standards should be aware of these issues. At the time of this writing, the NFPA 1001 Standard Committee is in the process of reevaluating the requirements throughout the standards and may make improvements in the fitness requirements section to remove any doubts concerning the test's validity.

The two topics I have discussed—medical standards and entry-level fitness standards—are important in recruit selection. At the same time, few if any volunteer departments require such standards. So you can be a "first" in your fire community. My purpose here is to encourage you to apply these standards, which your applicants must meet.

The purpose of this book is to provide you with better ideas for being an effective, innovative, and successful officer. You should know, then, how important health and fitness are to any firefighter's job, paid or volunteer. It takes only one chief to attack these problems that have been too long neglected in recruit selection. Work through your membership and your trustees or Board of Fire Commissioners. Establish both a medical and a fitness exam to keep from being "the first chief on your block" to lose a firefighter from a heart attack in the line of duty. If membership accepts your recommendations, it will be based largely on your strength of conviction in your ideas. You must make a firm decision and stand by it as you reassess the whole applicant process. For what it's worth, the American fire service considers physical fitness, as well as medical and physical entry standards, to be very important.

The Probationary Period

All the hard work that goes into recruiting and selecting good volunteers doesn't stop the moment that applicants are approved for membership. A good leader keeps a close watch on each and every new member's progress. The ultimate responsibility is yours.

Problems do come up. If, for instance, a new member doesn't understand what he should be doing under certain operations, such as high-rise procedures, and his station's line officer is not as available to help as he should be, then the new firefighter may be lost in the shuffle at the next high-rise fire. His fellow firefighters will wonder why he isn't following his assigned responsibilities under high-rise SOPs (standard operating procedures).

In the chapter on motivation and morale, I discussed an officer's responsibility to keep abreast of what's happening in every segment of his department. Problems at the onset for a new firefighter will adversely affect his motivation before he has really had a chance to experience life in the fire department.

You must work to monitor the weak and strong points of your new members. Make the chain of command work. Company officers should be the ones to start the communication process with the new member, if and when he is having problems. For you to step right in and intervene can undermine the very authority you have granted to those line officers. This does not mean that your attitude becomes one of "I don't want to hear about it until it becomes serious and you can't handle it." Every meeting you hold with the line officers should set aside some time to discuss the progress of each new member.

Keep a constant pulse on what is happening. And don't feel that the only thing that should be discussed is recruit *problems*. Find out where new members are doing well. The next time you see a new member who is doing well, make a point of making some encouraging remarks. It will do a lot for his morale and attitude.

The same goes for a chief officer. If you're pleased with the way a new firefighter is handling himself, take it as a sign that his lieutenant or captain is probably helping him along the way. A few positive words to your officer helps you too. It's the same old story of working up as well as down the chain of command.

Another way to monitor the probationary period is to design a "probationary performance" record. Include it in each new member's personnel file. Some of the areas to consider including are the following:

- Following orders from officers and performance on the fireground
- Performance during company trainings
- Interpersonal relations with other fire department members
- Nonfire duties: truck maintenance, house maintenance, fund drives, etc.
- Number of fire calls made for the month

You don't need a grading scale. Nevertheless, as each monthly line officer's meeting covers new members' progress, comments should be written on their performance record. If problems start to appear, you will likely catch them before they become serious.

Accountability

Accountability has become a common term in all facets of our working society. Each of us, for whatever professional and personal roles we accept responsibility, must bear the consequences of our actions. The public safety/emergency services field is, and always has been, held accountable by the public for responding to crisis situations. As an officer, you are a focal point when others praise or criticize the fire department's performance. If anyone is accountable, it is you.

Remember this when you think about new member orientation and the probationary period. Each new member must fully comprehend the seriousness of being a firefighter. As the individual progresses through his probationary period, you and your officers must clear up any misconception that being a volunteer means "not being accountable for anything." Drive home the point that every time a firefighter puts on his gear and steps on the runningboard or back step, he is immediately accountable for all his actions. Encourage any new recruit who has difficulty accepting this understanding to volunteer his services to another organization or community project.

When you make a serious tactical error in commanding a fireground operation, you can be sure that you'll hear about it. In fact, you should want it that way. If you didn't, it would encourage the stereotype that "they're only volunteers." Being accountable makes you comply with professional, competent standards of performance. Don't expect any more or any less of your men, both new and experienced, than you would of yourself. Accountability and competency, viewed in the right perspective, go hand in hand.

Profile of the Volunteer

I have talked at length on a systematic process to find the best applicants possible and turn them into good volunteer recruits. The more you know about your applicants, the better an assessment you'll make about whether certain men are right for the fire department, and the fire department is right for them.

There is one last subject worth discussing—the kinds of personalities attracted to volunteer firefighting. It's not talked about too often. But you should know why someone wants to join your fire department and serve under you. It affects your ability to command and manage effectively. Knowing those you lead will affect your relationships to and understanding of those people.

The personality types that generally want to join the volunteer fire service may include the following:

1. *The "I have time on my hands" volunteer.* This potential member may not have a job, may live alone or with his parents at home, and generally has no close peers. The fire department serves two

functions for him: (1) It's a place to spend a good part of his time when he doesn't have anywhere else to go; (2) it's a place to be around other people to whom he relates because of a common interest.
2. *The "Squad 51" volunteer.* This person wants to be a volunteer because he associates firefighting with an exciting image from the media: All firefighters are tough, they are *macho*. Television presents firefighting in glamorous but dangerous ways. Being a firefighter is the kind of stuff heroes are made of. Possibly this person feels the need to challenge his present life style with an activity that has a significant element of danger to it.
3. *The "authority figure" volunteer.* This volunteer is motivated by a false sense of authority. He overdecorates his car with emergency lights, if that's allowed in his particular jurisdiction, and he generally responds to an alarm by breaking the speed of sound. Everyone must get out of his way, for he holds the safety of the public in his hands. The sounds of the siren and air horn make him feel that he is the ultimate authority source from the time he gets in his car and responds to the station to the time he arrives at the fire scene. He speaks aggressively to his fellow firefighters or civilian bystanders. If you are the chief of a department, watch out for this kind of person. He can ruin any worthwhile image of an effective, efficient, courteous, mature, and professional firefighter under your command.
4. *The "I get turned on by firefighting" volunteer.* Firefighters understand the unusual feeling that comes when one is right in the midst of a big fire. The adrenalin starts flowing, and there is a tremendous feeling of excitement as you attack the fire head on. A psychiatrist could probably find some description for these emotions as being abnormal in behavior. But it is a unique feeling that only firefighters experience. There are, however, some who want to join the fire department because they really do get turned on by firefighting. They are go-getters, and when there's a slowdown of alarms, they might go out and create their own "activity"—making fires for the fire department to put out. One doesn't need a medical degree in psychiatry to realize how dangerous an individual like this can be to the entire community, let alone the fire department. Unfortunately, such deviant behavior often doesn't manifest itself until the person is actually in the department. The point here is, though you may not recognize these tendencies until

the person is actually in turnout gear, you should at least be aware that his type of personality is definitely attracted to the fire department. If he doesn't make it with you, he'll try somewhere else, perhaps with the rescue squad in town. He'll try to turn up anywhere there's excitement.

5. *The "public service minded" volunteer.* These are the individuals you want to have as members of your fire department, and they probably come closest to meeting your model criteria. Their desire to serve their community and neighbors, they feel, is best accomplished through the fire department. They are excited at the prospect of being firefighters and the adventure that goes with it. They will probably admit that. They not only feel that they can improve the level of public service in their community but they appreciate and respect firefighting as a dangerous yet challenging job. They are the men who may spend a good deal of time around the firehouse well before they become firefighters in your department, learning all they can about the job. Most of all, they tend to be mature, level-headed, and responsible individuals.

You can identify particular volunteers under your command who are dead-ringers for some of these personality types. Some of these volunteers, despite their undesirable personality characteristics, may be terrific firefighters on the fireground. They are useful members when the time calls for it. But, given a choice, the "public service minded" volunteer is the person you want to have in your department.

Understand that these personality types are certainly not the only people who become volunteers. You will also find that your applicants are a mix of these profiles. What is important is that you understand the kinds of people who are attracted to the volunteer fire department. You should know what motivates and drives them.

Some officers might contest these personality profiles by saying, "We can't afford to be choosy in an all-volunteer organization. We need members whenever and wherever we can get them." This is a dangerous posture to take. The truth of the matter is that you, the membership committee, and your general membership *can* afford to be selective. In fact, you are ethically derelict of duty if you select applicants who fall far short of your qualifications.

You owe it to yourself as an officer to see to it that any new member demonstrates the potential to work effectively, with a cool head, as a representative of your fire department. You and the members owe that much to the community you serve and protect. If the community's opinion is of little concern, you at least owe it to yourselves.

Just picture yourself in a working structural fire making a search for victims. Who would you want as your backup or partner, should you need help—the "authority figure" volunteer or the "public service minded" volunteer? As an officer, you are entrusted with the health and welfare of thousands of people, not to mention the protection of millions of dollars' worth of property. The capability of the men serving under your command reflects on you and the way you run your department. If you take any pride in your effort to be an excellent fire officer, you will be selective about who fights fires for you in your town. You don't have to settle for just a warm body.

Notes

1. Paul C. Ditzel, *Fire Engines, Firefighters* (New York: Crown, 1976), p. 28.
2. International Association of Fire Fighters 1978 Annual Death and Injury Survey.
3. *International Association of Fire Fighters Mortality Report* (Washington, D.C.: National Fire Prevention and Control Administration, 1976).
4. "Death and Injury Statistics in the Line of Duty," *Fire Command*, May 1979.
5. Paul O. Davis and Major Howell F. Wright, "Elements of a Recruit Selection Process," *Fire Command*, January, 1979.

> *Every fire officer must realize that all facets of the fire service are being closely scrutinized in the legal circles. People are willing to bring suit if there is the slightest hint of negligence. Remember: your next fire suppression operation may be critiqued in a court of law.*
>
> —THOMAS M. HAWKINS, JR., FORMER CHIEF,
> VIENNA VOLUNTEER
> FIRE DEPARTMENT,
> VIENNA, VIRGINIA

8 / *Legal Liabilities*

Today's volunteer officer has many roles other than fireground commander. He must be a manager, coordinator, public relations spokesman, planner, recruiter, and trainer. Each role has its own special dimensions.

There's an additional role that's becoming more important for the volunteer fire officer: that of legal specialist. I don't mean that a volunteer officer should be a law school graduate. But I do think he should think about the potential legal consequences of his job.

America's courts are replete with civil suits, sometimes even criminal cases, in which one party claims some injustice has been committed against him or her. If there's any truth to the growing popular belief that defendants are now considered guilty until proven innocent, then any potentially liable individual or group ought to know the realities.

The general public usually appreciates the fine work that volunteer firefighters do. But don't be fooled. Doing noble deeds such as protecting life and property from fire doesn't make a chief immune from legal liability. Moreover, the chances are strong that a chief and his department can be sued for nonfighting as well as firefighting duties.

This chapter discusses various events that may make an officer vulnerable to litigation. Though I hope nothing like this will ever happen to you, and that you plan against any such eventuality, you must still be prepared.

Telling you about the legal risks is only half the job. This chapter also discusses practical preventative measures that will reduce the probability of a chief and his fire department becoming defendants in the courtroom.

Situation 1: Physical Requirements and Standards

Volunteer fire department applicants are rarely required to meet specified physical performance standards. Yet statistics from the National Fire Protection Association showed that volunteers in 1978 suffered a higher degree of cardiovascular disease through heart attacks than did their paid counterparts. Keep in mind that heart attack accounts for practically 50 percent of firefighter deaths in the line of duty; this too, has been substantiated through research. There are great risks in being a firefighter. Nevertheless, the fire service has an obligation to reduce significantly as many controllable risk factors as possible. It's also the chief's obligation because he can in part control the physical well-being of his firefighters.

Various exercise physiologists and medical doctors have long told us about the risk factors of heart disease and firefighting. They are (1) lack of physical activity (specifically cardiovascular exercise), (2) elevated blood fats, (3) smoking, (4) obesity, (5) stress, (6) hypertension (elevated blood pressure), and (7) heredity. Of all these factors, only one is totally uncontrollable—heredity. All the others can be treated or modified to some degree.

What are the legal issues? To begin with, a volunteer who dies from a heart attack not caused by toxic smoke poisoning may have had a history of high blood pressure and high cholesterol levels. If he left a family or other dependents, some of them may wonder why he was doing such a dangerous task in the first place. If the chief didn't know about the firefighter's health problems, because he never took the time to find out about them, he could be held liable for the man's death.

Suggested Preventative Actions

Be more demanding about the physical standards for all department members. These standards are justified because identifying physical problems can prevent physically unfit applicants from ever becoming firefighters.

First, each applicant should have his blood pressure checked for hypertension. Any applicant with 140/90 or higher should see a physician for further examination. It costs virtually nothing to check a patient's blood pressure. The nurse in a town health department can do it. So can any EMTs in the fire department or township rescue squad.

Second, require a blood chemistry workup for any highly qualified applicant. For a nominal fee, a reputable medical laboratory can tell the levels of HDL (high density lipoproteins), cholesterol, and triglycerides, all of which are critical measures in potential heart disease.

Third, administer a valid physical performance test consisting of predictor-type tests. Firefighting requires high aerobic capacity, muscular strength, and muscular endurance. Test measures such as a mile-and-a-half run, push-ups, and sit-ups are all predictors of these physical attributes. Make it mandatory that an applicant pass this exam in order to be accepted for probationary status.

These are demanding requirements for volunteers. Nevertheless, set these standards and keep others from pointing the finger at you later, saying, "Didn't you know that he had high blood pressure and shouldn't have been a firefighter?"

A few words of caution: If you do administer a physical performance test, state all the requirements in writing and make them publicly available to anyone interested. Also, any applicant wanting to take the test should (1) have at least one month's notice of when the test will be given and (2) sign a waiver absolving the fire department of any blame in the event of health complications from the tests (e.g., having chest pains after the mile-and-a-half run).

Institute a voluntary physical fitness program for all cur-

rently active members. Try to get the donated services of an exercise physiologist to help set up the program. It's very difficult to make fitness programs mandatory, though they really should be, even as firefighters are expected to obey all SOPs and fire department rules and regulations. Nonetheless, it's still difficult in a volunteer fire department to force this kind of program. Perhaps, by educating the volunteers they will realize that high levels of physical performance are important on the job.

Situation 2: Applicant Discrimination

This is one issue that doesn't need much introduction. We are all aware of federal legislation mandating equal employment opportunities for women and minorities. The volunteer fire department is not a place of employment, and because it isn't it does not fall under the same regulations that would exist if a minority group member or a woman was not given the same opportunity as a white male to be a paid firefighter. But your department is accountable to state and federal laws on discrimination if some portion of its operating expenses, however small, are dispersed through revenue-sharing funds that eventually reach the municipal level.

Assuming that you have an applicant you don't want in your department—not on the basis of race/color/creed/national origin but for what you consider to be nondiscriminatory reasons—and the applicant is either a woman or a member of a minority group, how can you sustain the rejection and not be vulnerable to a civil action?

SUGGESTED PREVENTATIVE ACTIONS

Use a membership application form that gives you essential and detailed information about the applicant. It shouldn't have any questions that are considered discriminatory in nature. Consult your department's legal counsel and get his or her professional judgment on the potential problems with your application form.

Make certain that any standards for acceptance or rejection are nondiscriminatory, valid, and fair for all. An example is the female who wants to be a volunteer. The fire service has traditionally been a men's haven, and there's been slow progress in expanding the firefighting job to women. A typical excuse to a woman firefighter is that "she doesn't have the physical capability to perform the job." This may be totally untrue.

A woman who is a nonsmoker, exercises on a regular basis, has low blood cholesterol, normal blood pressure, and possesses a high level of aerobic fitness, muscular strength, muscular endurance, and lean body mass, with low levels of fat weight, is a far better physical risk than a male who fails on these factors. These are valid measures or standards.

But to ask a 5'4" woman to take a ground ladder off the side of an engine and reject her because she cannot reach it is a risk action. That task is not a valid predictor of physical capability in a firefighter, and an informed exercise physiologist, one who deals with public safety personnel health and fitness, will know it.

Whatever standards or regulations exist in your fire department's bylaws on accepting or rejecting applicants should apply equally to all applicants. Your manpower needs may be greatest in the daytime. So you start recruiting shift workers, and given two equally qualified candidates, the shift worker gets preference. That membership requirement, even if it's temporary, is fine as long as it applies to all applicants. The minute a female or minority candidate, who happens to be a shift worker, is not accepted, but another applicant who works only in the daytime is, you have violated the conditions of equal opportunity.

Situation 3: Firefighter/Fire Officer Training and Certification

We may well be saying good-bye to the days when a volunteer fire department used poor fire-suppression strategies and tactics, lost the entire structure (or a good portion if it) and possibly a life, and the worst that people said was, "Well, they're only volunteers. They did the best they could." The favorite term these days is accountability, and it's a word that's not far away from liability.

The American insurance industry has raised premiums so much in recent years that it's not unusual to see them go up each time you file a claim. Moreover, no smart person purchases a home or starts a business without sufficient fire insurance coverage, because a fire can bring financial ruin.

Are you prepared to be in court someday as the defendant in a civil action that challenges the decisions you made at a fire scene? How will you handle accusations from plaintiff's counsel that you, as chief, were derelict in duty, that you didn't protect exposures and caused a property loss of thousands of dollars? Even worse, how will you defend an accusation that someone died because your firefighters did not carry out proper rescue procedures in attempting to save the victim? Be prepared for any accusations.

SUGGESTED PREVENTATIVE ACTIONS

As an officer, you bear the ultimate responsibility for what your firefighters do at a fire, and for any others under your command when neighboring companies assist at a mutual-aid alarm. First and foremost, make training a very high priority—and this means more than just interdepartmental training. Send your firefighters to as many state, regional, and federal training programs as possible. It shows that you're working to maintain and upgrade the fire-suppression command skills of you and your officers. Sure, you can attend numerous training programs and still make a serious mistake at a fire scene. But the more formal training you and your officers have, the less chance that you or they will make poor decisions in strategy and deploying manpower. It's definitely a safeguard against accusations that your formal training isn't enough to meet a chief's responsibilities.

Institute as many formalized training standards within your department as possible. For instance, try a "smoke divers" program where any volunteer donning self-contained breathing apparatus has completed an extensive and difficult qualification program. There are still volunteer departments that give new and inexperienced members protective equipment and let them respond on the apparatus without ever having completed and passed a tough orientation program. These are dangerous risks to take. Any new volunteer should be able to explain and/or demonstrate where all equipment is located on the engine, ladder truck, rescue unit, or ambulance; how to use protective gear and self-contained breathing apparatus properly; all fire department SOPs and other related rules and regulations; how to use all essential firefighting equipment properly. And the volunteer should know these things *before* he sets foot on the apparatus.

Know the latest fire protection/prevention/management issues. Subscribing to all the major fire service magazines is one way to do this. These magazines publish essential information. Read them on a regular basis. You will be familiar with what other fire officers across the country are doing to maintain high professional standards.

Either start or build upon a reference library. By getting the publications listings each year from such organizations as the National Fire Protection Association and the Robert J. Brady Company, recognized publishers of fire service texts, you can add new books yearly that will help you do a better job of leading and commanding.

Doing the best job you can works most of the time. Yet, if challenged, you want to be able to defend your actions and decisions. The way to do this is with formal, professional, and continuous training and knowledge.

Situation 4: Injuries and Medical Evaluation

We know that the risks of getting injured or killed are high in firefighting. That holds true for volunteers as well as paid firefighters. The death of three volunteer firefighters in a swimming pool chemicals store explosion in Bethpage, New York, a fire set by an arsonist in 1978, is testimony to that.

From the time you become an officer until the time you leave office, you'll hope that there will never be a member lost in the line of duty in your department. But there are certain to be injuries to volunteers, and some of them will be serious. If you're in command, you want to treat all injuries as serious. It's too easy to be lax about an injury. Don't gamble.

SUGGESTED PREVENTATIVE ACTIONS

Make it clear that any injury sustained at a fire call, even if it's minor, must be reported to an officer and noted in the report. If you have any doubts, play it safe and have the volunteer see a physician as soon as possible. In addition, place the volunteer on sick leave pending a doctor's release or statement that the injury will in no way inhibit the volunteer's ability to perform all expected duties on the fireground.

Thoroughly question the injured volunteer about the accident. Find out if the injury can be related to any particular action at the fire scene. If it is related, then make it a point to train all your firefighters against making that same mistake again. You are doing your job by recording the incident and requiring a medical examination. But you're not doing your job well if you allow the same accident to happen a second time because no action was taken the first time. From a liability standpoint, you'll be in better shape if you can find a lesson to be learned from an unfortunate incident.

Reinforcing proper firematic skills for new and inexperienced volunteers is a must. This may sound too simple. Yet an excellent research study, the *Firefighter Mortality Report*, of the International Association of Firefighters, studied causes leading to line-of-duty deaths of firefighters. In some cases, death resulted from inexperience and a lack of recent familiarity with special skills. In the first instance, inexperienced young firefighters made mistakes that proved serious. They had gone through recruit training, yet had encountered a situation in which they could not rely on past experience to guide their judgment and actions. In the second instance, the firefighters/officers were experienced veterans. But given, for example, a captain who had been in an engine company for the past eight years and then was transferred to a truck company, his forgetting some proper truck company procedures caused a judgmental error that proved fatal. This is understandable when you consider the dangerous task of search and rescue above and on the fire floor, a job for all truck company firefighters.

Situation 5: Emergency Driving

In 1979 the New York State Supreme Court's Appellate Division ruled that violation of the speeding rules by an ambulance driver constituted misconduct. Furthermore, a claimant would not be eligible to receive unemployment compensation if fired from his or her job because of such a violation.

The case involved an ambulance driver in Rochester, New York. He was charged with driving 48 and 55 miles an hour in a 30-mile-per-hour zone. He did this knowing that his employer had set regulations against exceeding the speed limit, even in emergencies. Acknowledging his awareness of the rule, the driver nonetheless felt he was exempted from it because of the nature of the call.

One of the fundamental premises of prehospital emergency medical care is to stabilize a patient's condition before transport and then drive at a reasonable, safe speed. However, some EMS experts believe that if EMS personnel are responding to known emergencies, such as respiratory and cardiac arrest, and they are first responders on the scene, they might be accused of not responding quickly enough. It's possible that the patient or the patient's family could sue the fire department or private ambulance service because they were convinced that the delay caused by driving at normal speeds contributed to the patient's serious condition.

This incident concerned an ambulance driver. The circumstances might differ, but the same type of situation could happen to a volunteer driver/pump operator and his fire department. Laws can be quite specific about driving to emergency scenes by emergency personnel. And the liability risks here are great.

What regulations have you mandated on the driving practices of your volunteers, in their own automobiles as well as on the apparatus? Do different driving rules exist for different emergency calls in your department's regulations?

SUGGESTED PREVENTATIVE ACTIONS

What does communication have to do with driving? More than you might think. The more precise information on the nature of the call, the greater discretion the driver and engine/truck/ambulance officer can exercise while responding.

An important responsibility of any volunteer chief is to establish as functional and effective a communication system as possible. One reason for this is that volunteers should respond to some other message than "you have a call." What kind of call? Is there a life risk? Does the driver need to respond immediately, or can he proceed at a speed closer to the speed limit, knowing the nature of the call?

Imagine the legal consequences of hearing that "you have a fire call" and responding on the assumption that it is a working fire, whereas the alarm turns out to be a kitchen odor of smoke. You can almost write the courtroom transcript with the judge asking you why your volunteers caused a serious auto accident while responding at high speeds to a minor fire call.

Communication is important. It will help you better enforce your rules concerning emergency driving.

Establish and enforce regulations for all conceivable driving circumstances. I'm sure that your department does this already. However, you should review your procedure from time to time.

First, what are the state laws for volunteers driving to the station or directly to the fire scene? Have they changed recently, or are there any state bills pending that may change existing laws? If a volunteer has an accident and causes bodily injury to people, he will not only be liable for the motor vehicle violation he commits—the fire department also may be liable. As long as you enforce state, municipal, and fire department rules, and you use judgment and discretion with each circumstance, your protection base is firm.

As for driving emergency vehicles, all pump operators should demonstrate to your satisfaction a competent ability to operate the apparatus. This is especially important for large apparatus such as aerial ladders, ladder towers, squirts, or snorkels. It would be wise to have the municipality administer special eye examinations for all drivers to test such critical factors as depth perception. A driver who has serious vision deficiencies may be more prone to have an accident.

Have an officer, a veteran skilled driver, or both, attend a formal training course on operating emergency vehicles and defensive driving. Once they learn the essential skills of driving emergency vehicles properly under all circumstances, they can then train the other drivers in the department.

To make the most of this training, plan on sending personnel on a regular basis, possibly every two or three years. You'll be keeping current on the newest and recommended driving skills for emergency vehicles.

Situation 6: Disciplinary Charges and Dismissal

We can't always select the best applicants. A member may not turn out to be as committed as you would have liked. He's a marginal performer, doing what is required and nothing more. This is a reality that exists in all organizations.

It's more serious when the volunteer goes one step further. He is now being disciplined, possibly for disobeying orders, accusations of stealing fire department property, or responding on fire apparatus while under the influence of alcohol or drugs. The actions are serious enough that he could be dropped from the department rolls.

The way you handle it, however, can result in prompt action or endless complications. A poorly handled dismissal proceeding may return to haunt you through a civil suit. Specifically, a member who is charged and subsequently dismissed for stealing fire department property may legally counter the action, stating that the evidence was insufficient, that he was not afforded due process under the bylaws of the organizational charter, and that he should not be denied membership privileges. Let's discuss how to guard against this.

SUGGESTED PREVENTATIVE ACTIONS

It takes only a poor fire department leader with a strong following to abuse the written rules of the organization. This situation is dangerous, and if it exists in your department, put a stop to it. Your department's bylaws should be written and modified as needed to establish fairness and equality for everyone in all situations and circumstances. But they can be misused. Policy systems in most organizational settings are sound. The problem is that the system is mismanaged by people. Therefore, any fire department member who is under investigation should have the chance for due process to answer all charges before a reviewing body of impartial judges. You and your fire department will then be fulfilling its obligations and responsibility under your system of regulations.

Any charges brought against a member that could end in dismissal must be fully substantiated. This holds true if a member is accused of either stealing or destroying fire department property. If you and the fire department president decide to press criminal charges against the member, you must have valid evidence—irrefutable evidence—that the illegal act did in fact take place and that the accused member was the culprit.

If the situation actually goes as far as a court proceeding, the accused ex-member will be in public view. Your inability to verify charges may lead to a dismissal of the charges, and the judge has the right to order the member reinstated in the fire department.

The hypothetical story does not end here. What's to keep the member from filing a civil suit against you and the rest of the fire department for defamation of character? In addition, one well-placed phone call to the local newspapers will give you and the department the kind of publicity you want to avoid at all costs.

Be sure before you accuse anyone. The repercussions can be much more severe than you or anyone else in the department guessed they could be.

Situation 7: Fire Incident Reports

This is one of the most important situations. The written fire incident report, especially the narrative section, is the most reliable record of events that a chief or other officer has.

It's not unusual to be called into a courtroom as a witness or a defendant two or three years after a fire has resulted in litigation. How will you remember everything that happened three years ago? If you did not include an extensive narrative of the events of the firefighting operation, how will you remember specific details? If you're unfortunate enough to be the defendant, the decisions you made and the operations you commanded will be the facts that lawyers or judges will use to decide any level of negligence.

Suggested Preventative Actions

All facts and information related to the fire operation, even though they are checked off or listed on the incident fact sheet, should be repeated in the narrative report. Every fact—time of alarm, weather conditions, all equipment and apparatus used, conditions that existed when decisions were made to ventilate, charge hand lines, cut off gas and electricity, when firefighters entered the structure, why, and to what purposes—must be fully described and explained. In essence, I'm talking about a story, complete with every fact and detail from start to finish, no matter how insignificant the point may seem at the time.

Avoid any affirmative statement where you are making a judgment as to the fire cause if you have not been formally trained and qualified to make those judgments, especially to make them so that they will hold up in a court of law. A good example is an attic fire caused by an improperly installed attic vent fan with thermostatic control. After the fire has been knocked down, the chief and some of his officers may inspect the electrical wiring to the fan and see that it was neither properly installed nor complied with the municipal electrical code.

They might be 85 percent right in their assessment. If they have not been formally trained in electrical wiring code enforcement and inspection, however, they are not qualified to make such judgments. Moreover, the assessment should not be mentioned in the report. It's one thing to describe conditions or events; it's quite another to make assumptions based on legally unrecognized judgment.

Another instance is when firefighters discover evidence that could categorize the fire as incendiary. The evidence may be obvious—a gasoline can, lots of soaked rags, an accelerant trail on the floor, and fire determined to have been in as many as three separate locations. This does not mean that the fire report should *not* state any reference to arson. It should certainly state this fact if firefighters and officers had formal training in arson detection and preserved the evidence as they were taught to do. But nothing should be said that infers that it was an incendiary fire, as judged by the firefighters.

There's a world of difference between arson detection and arson investigation. If you have completed arson investigation training and investigate suspicious fires on a regular basis, you have some legitimate reason for making such statements in the report. If you haven't been trained, then leave the judgments to qualified investigators. The statements about arson should appear in their report, not in yours.

Situation 8: Authorized Fireground Responsibilities

You know the geographical boundaries of your fire protection area. If your department protects all property in your town, then there's no mistaking how far you can go—to the boundary lines of the town. If more than one fire department serves your town, however, then you and the other chief(s) must agree on specified protection areas.

There are risks to crossing the line of fire protection responsibility from yours to another area, either in your town or out of it. What happens if you and your firefighters actively fight a fire in another town, and you later get sued for the way you commanded your part of the operation? What if one of your firefighters gets injured on a mutual-aid response? What happens if you decide to withdraw your firefighters from a mutual-aid call because you disagree with the existing operation?

SUGGESTED PREVENTATIVE ACTIONS

Require written agreements between your department and any others outside your protection area. These agreements should state the conditions under which your department will be called to assist. It should also state that you and your department will not be liable to a legal action, criminal or civil, because of any action and decisions taken and made by you at that fire.

You may think that all this sounds formal and unnecessary. And to ask for a written agreement with another department where you have had an oral agreement for years may be difficult at first. But it's in your best interests.

If there is a county mutual-aid system, that system should also be backed by a written policy of who does what, when, and where—and who is responsible, ultimately and legally.

Establish a written agreement that covers you, your department, and municipal leaders in the kinds of emergencies to which your department will respond. This is a side track of the original situation—responsibilities outside your protection area. But you're just as vulnerable in your own area.

Insist that the kinds of fire/rescue calls your firefighters respond to are specifically stated in an official document. Essentially, you're agreeing to provide certain services, understanding that you can be legally responsible for your decision and actions at that emergency call. If you don't get stray animals out of trees, then the agreement should state that you don't. And if your department does not fill swimming pools or empty septic tanks, it should say that also.

As I stated in my introduction to this chapter, my purpose is not to make you a lawyer. My purpose is to identify some of the increasingly vulnerable areas that make an officer prone to liability. Your capacity to plan against such occurrences, regardless of how remote they seem, is and will continue to be a valuable asset to your managerial skills. Too few officers think about these issues until after the fact. Then they don't need this book; they need an attorney. Let that be one event in your command that will never take place.

> *No longer can we just "throw water through the window." Advanced technologies breed complex fires that confront us with situations requiring professional judgment and skill. Training is the key that will unlock the solution to these situations and allow the volunteer fire service to meet the demands placed upon it.*
> —WILLIAM SICKLES, FORMER CHIEF,
> MASSAPEQUA VOLUNTEER
> FIRE DEPARTMENT,
> MASSAPEQUA, NEW YORK

9 / The Training Function

The officer's goal in firefighting is to control and extinguish the fire. He accomplishes part of his task through effective field command. Another part entails how much planning he's done in deploying manpower and apparatus at the scene. The greatest part of the goal, however, is the speed and efficiency with which his firefighters use the skills taught them to accomplish fire control and extinguishment.

I'm talking about many skills: ventilation, where to place master streams, positioning of first-due engines and trucks, forcible entry, engine company hose evolutions, use and placement of ladders, proper donning of self-contained breathing apparatus, foam application, search and rescue operations, salvage, overhaul, control of hazardous material spills, and so on.

Learning hands-on skills is not the final process. We learn ideas and theories through tactics and strategies, and these give some meaning to our skills. An example is when the first engine or truck arrives at a working structure fire. The officer's training has taught him to make the following assessments:

- Is there a life hazard?
- Where is the fire and where did it originate?
- Are there exposure hazards?
- Must I vent the building right away?

The Training Function

- What problems will weather conditions present?
- When can I expect the second-due units, especially if this is a daytime fire and manpower is low?
- Where should I make my initial hand-line attack to begin fire control?
- Do I need to transmit a second alarm or request mutual aid, depending on my available manpower and the progression of the fire?

Based on decisions to act or not act on these judgments, the officer orders his firefighters to perform certain tasks. Their ability to perform those tasks skillfully and efficiently, combined with the officer's size-up, ultimately determines how well they control the fire.

We gain the ability to control a situation through training. Training has been one of the formidable mainstays of the fire service since its beginnings. In many ways, training has taken on new levels of sophistication, finally incorporating some contemporary trends found in corporate business training and development. But in other ways, firefighter training has shown little progress over the years.

One area in which there's been little change is the volunteer service. The problem is not that officers aren't teaching skills to firefighters. The problem is that they don't place enough emphasis on some important components of learning: measurable, performance-based objectives; the "classroom" setting; effective and varied instructional styles; planning training lessons; measuring training effectiveness; instructor evaluation; and simulation.

These topics sound complicated, but in fact they aren't. They are basically simple in concept, and when properly incorporated into a training program for volunteers, they help both officers and firefighters reach their goal of efficient and successful fire control.

You cannot change your training regimen overnight. With each phase you will go through the steps of learning the teaching skill, experimenting with it, evaluating what went well and what didn't, reexperimenting, reevaluating, and finally making that skill part of each officer's training techniques. Little by little, though, officers of the department will see how these skills in training can significantly improve on the information their firefighters are getting and putting into action.

Training by Performance-Based Objectives

Ideally, you want each training session to be interesting and informative. The firefighters should know more than they did when they came into the class. The question is, How will you know if they do? How does an officer really know whether he succeeded in teaching the volunteers what he set out to teach? Did a volunteer think that he learned some point the instructor made when, in fact, his understanding of the information wasn't at all what the officer was trying to convey?

In the fire department, we see this problem manifest itself on the fireground. For example, the captain of the department holds a Saturday morning training session on hydraulics for all pump operators. His purpose is to improve their skill in discharging the proper water pressure for operating multiple hand lines off an engine. He has taught this particular training lesson before.

The reason for this training session is not so much for review as it is a response to complaints. Firefighters have been complaining that drivers are not doing a good job of regulating discharge pressures on 1½-inch and 1¾-inch hand lines. Nozzle pressures, they say, either tend to be too low or too high. The chief feels that the situation is serious enough to warrant some special training before taking steps to requalify all drivers. The captain is assigned the training.

So the captain and the pump operators meet on Saturday. The captain gives a lecture on calculating the proper engine pressure, based on hose length, friction loss, hose diameter, and GPM (gallons per minute) setting at the nozzle, to arrive at the proper nozzle pressure. He lectures while everyone stands around the pump panel and the engine is hooked to a hydrant with three 1½-inch lines coming off, all of different lengths. After the lecture, the captain goes through a practical demonstration of charging all three lines, setting the desired nozzle pressure on the longest line, and gating down the other two. The pump operators are asked to do the calculations, and the captain does the actual demonstration.

Three weeks later, there is a working fire, and the first-due engine on the scene is operating lines off all four discharge gates. The engine had laid in a line from a hydrant, and the second-due engine had picked up the line and was now the water source from the hydrant.

After the fire is under control, a few of the firefighters come up to the captain and again complain about the pressures on their lines. Some say that it was too much and that the line was too hard to control. Others complain that the pressure was too low and was totally ineffective against the fire, jeopardizing their safety when they were close to the flames.

The captain is puzzled. He cannot understand why the pump operators haven't learned anything from their training. He lectured them on the whole process and then demonstrated how they should do it. Since he is the captain, and he understands how it's done, he decides the problem must be theirs. Either they are slow learners or they just weren't paying attention.

Yes, it might be their problem. But it could also be his.

Keep this story in mind while we discuss performance-based learning objectives. To begin with, no officer should start a training session without a list of objectives to be met— objectives that ensure all firefighters will learn what they're supposed to. It is necessary to differentiate between a "goal" and an "objective." A goal is the desire to reach a long-range plan. An example of a goal is the following:

One goal of the Bakerstown Volunteer Fire Department is to improve the level of fire protection significantly for all citizens by the year 1990.

This statement relates something that the fire department hopes to accomplish in the future. Because it is a goal, it does not specifically state how this improved level of fire protection will be achieved. In 1990, the number of working fires may be higher, but the firefighter's skills may also be improved. An observer might interpret the increase in fires as indicating a poor level of fire protection in town. Even though this isn't necessarily the case, the goal set down by the Bakerstown department is not stated in measurable terms. So who can determine whether the fire protection level has improved or not?

In contrast to this, an objective is and should be stated in measurable terms. An example of an objective is the following:

By the end of one year's time, and given financial assistance from the township, 65 percent of the 60 active volunteers in the Bakerstown Volunteer Fire Department will have completed the NFPA Firefighter II training program. Successful completion of the program will require attendance at all sessions and passing scores of 80 percent or better on both the final written and practical exams.

What makes this a performance-based objective? How does it really differ from the previously stated goal? Here's how.

1. *The objective is clearly stated.* An objective must be stated clearly. No one should have any questions about it. In our sample objective the Bakerstown volunteers clearly understand that their officers want at least 65 percent of them to complete Firefighter II by the end of one year. It is also clear what they must do to pass the course successfully and qualify for certification.
2. *The objective must be achievable.* An objective is different from a goal because an objective is realistic and achievable. For instance, knowing that there is money available to pay for training and one year's time to accomplish it, it is quite realistic that 65 percent of Bakerstown's active volunteers can complete the program. It would become unrealistic if the time limitation was reduced to three months. In that time, maybe only 30 percent of the volunteers could complete the training.
3. *The objective must be measurable.* In addition to being achievable, an objective must be measurable. Then you will know whether you met it or not. If we were to say that the objective was for 65 percent of all volunteers to understand the Firefighter II requirements, how would we measure their "understanding"? In-

stead, the objective states that 65 percent must complete the course by achieving minimum scores to pass. So we know what to measure to determine whether the objective has been met. "Understand" is not a measurable term, whereas "successfully pass," given specific standards, is.

One technique that some people use to write a performance-based objective is the "A-B-C-D Method." This system, developed through the U.S. Department of Education, breaks down an objective into four parts.

A—Audience. The specific group that is performing the task and reaching the objective is clearly defined. In this case, it is all active volunteers in Bakerstown.
B—Behavior. Behavior refers to what the identified audience will be doing to achieve the objective. Completion of NFPA Firefighter II by 65 percent of all active Bakerstown volunteers is the desired behavior.
C—Conditions. This describes the limitations or parameters set down for the objective. Our example states a condition of one year's time to complete the program, as well as financial assistance to pay for the training. Other conditions can be the time of day, the site where behavior will take place, the specific equipment available to perform the action, and so on.
D—Degree. Degree refers to the requirements the performer must meet to be successful. The active Bakerstown volunteers understand that they must reach minimum scores on the written and practical tests to pass Firefighter II.

These four components differentiate an objective from a goal. The component "degree" is not always necessary, but every objective must possess a defined audience, behavior, or outcome, and conditions for the action to take place.

The Classroom Setting

A fire officer may spend considerable time planning a training session. He wants to make sure that his firefighters really learn something. First, he decides what to teach in the lesson. Second, he establishes some measurable objectives to find out if the firefighters really learned what they should have learned.

This is all fine so far. There are other considerations, though, in making this particular training session effective. One important consideration is the classroom setting.

I'm talking about classroom setting as an environment in which students can learn easily. This environment may be indoors or outdoors. Whichever, certain conditions must exist for the learning process to be meaningful. What are these circumstances, and how do they affect training?

1. *Proximity to the instructor.* A training officer should make sure that all his firefighters can both clearly see and hear him during the training session. If the firefighters cannot do one or the other, they may not understand or may even totally miss an important point in the lesson. Though we like to say that there is no such thing as a stupid question, someone will miss something but won't say anything for fear of being embarrassed.

    It's up to the training officer to arrange his class so that everyone hears what he says and sees what he demonstrates. This should be done at the start of the class, before the presentation begins.

2. *Avoiding distractions.* A good lesson can run a strong second to unnecessary interference. The more distractions there are, the more difficult it will be for anyone to concentrate on what is being taught.

    An excellent example of this is an outside training session taught either near a busy highway or some other loud disturbance. However interesting the training session is, and however much the firefighters respect the officer conducting the lesson, they cannot help but be distracted by the interfering noises. Here is some advice on handling this problem.

    a. The firefighters should face away from any distractions. The training officer should face any distractions. By doing this, the firefighters won't be tempted to let their eyes wander. Also, if the distraction is behind them, they won't turn around to see it because it will look as if they're not paying attention and cause them embarrassment.

b. Obviously, avoid either indoor or outdoor locations where distractions are likely to occur. This is all part of effective planning for the training session. It may be noise, it may be the weather, it may be the time of day. Regardless, plan accordingly and eliminate as many distractions as possible.
3. *Student comfort.* When the learning environment is comfortable for the student, it helps the learning process. Being uncomfortable makes us think more about the discomfort than about what we're being taught. For instance, the training officer may be conducting a lesson on hydraulics for pump operators. In the first part of the lesson, he lectures on how to calculate engine pressures, friction loss, nozzle pressures, elevation, and so on; the second part of the lesson is actually trying all these procedures. The training officer is smart to hold the first part of the class indoors where all pump operators can sit comfortably and he can use a blackboard to demonstrate the calculations. Then everyone can go out on the apparatus to a location, drop some line, and practice what has been taught.

   If the training officer were to teach the training class outside, the pump operators would be standing around while he discussed hydraulic principles and calculations. They could as easily have done that inside. All they got from standing around was fatigue.
4. *Needed materials.* If the training officer is planning a problem-solving exercise such as how to fight a hypothetical fire as part of prefire planning, he's going to need certain materials. For example, each firefighter will get more value out of the exercise if the fire situation is presented on a diagramed paper for each person to read and refer to. It would be far less effective if the situation were described verbally. Think in the following terms:
   a. Do I have paper, pencils, and a blackboard, if needed, for an indoor session?
   b. Is the apparatus set up or equipped the way I want it if I am practicing evolutions outdoors and I want certain things to happen?
   c. Are there enough materials to go around so that everyone is active instead of having the majority waiting for two people to get done? For example, Are there 2 ropes for 20 firefighters to practice tying knots?

Teaching Methods

An important part of the educational process is using a variety of teaching methods. In past years teachers of all kinds have believed that lecture was the only way that people learned: "You listen, and I will tell you." The fire service has practiced that method of teaching in its training for many years.

I'm not saying that the lecture method is bad or unproductive, because it isn't. On the other hand, we have learned that different teaching styles, varied effectively, can have a positive effect on the learning process. This should be especially true when the way a firefighter learns and gets information directly affects his decisions and actions on the fireground. If he learns well, what he learns may someday save his life.

I want to clear up one thing. As teaching moves away from the lecture method, it generally places more decision-making responsibility on the learner and less on the teacher. This gives the teacher or trainer more time to go around and talk with students. He can make sure that they really are learning as they make more decisions. Several teaching methods can be considered.

The Lecture

The lecture has traditionally been the most used teaching method in the fire service. The fire department is a paramilitary organization; it always has been. Part of reinforcing the officer/firefighter distinction is through training sessions where the officers are the experts. They teach; firefighters listen.

The lecture method is best for you and other officers when the material you teach is new to your firefighters and many fine points need to be covered. A lecture is the fastest way to transmit that information to them.

One drawback to using lectures alone is that the training officer has no way of knowing whether all the students understood what they learned until he sees them use that knowledge or those skills at a fire. Lectures are fine for presenting new information. But they need to be reinforced by other learning experiences to let the training officer know that he succeeded in his presentation. If he doesn't have any follow-up activity, such as a written test, then he can only *assume* that they all learned what he wanted them to.

TASK LEARNING

Let's say that the training officer has just lectured on three totally new ways for one person to carry a 50-foot length of hose back to the apparatus for packing. None of the firefighters has ever seen these methods before. After the training officer lectures on the techniques and demonstrates how each carry is done, he tells each firefighter to take a 50-foot length of 2½-inch line and begin practicing the three carries.

By assigning them these tasks, the officer accomplishes the following:

1. Each firefighter makes a decision for himself as to where he is going to practice the tasks, how often he will do them, and how fast he will do them. He is making decisions on his own.
2. The training officer can walk around to each individual volunteer and actually see whether that person understands the three new carries. This contact between training officer and volunteer acts as a check to see if proper learning is taking place. If the volunteer is correct, the officer can reinforce it; if he's wrong, the officer can correct him right away.

RECIPROCAL INSTRUCTION

This teaching method goes a step farther in expanding the decision-making process for the learner. Reciprocal instruction requires two people working together. One has the role of the performer, and the other enacts the evaluator.

Here's what takes place. After the training officer tells everyone the correct steps for performing each hose carry, the performer goes through his practice of the different carries. The observer, concentrating on how the carries are supposed to be done, comments to the performer. By closely watching, the observer tells his partner what he was doing correctly on the carries, as well as what was incorrect and needs to be changed. This method also serves as a learning experience for the observer because his view of what is and should be the way to do the task reinforces his own knowledge. After the task is completed, the performer and observer switch roles.

What is the training officer doing during all of this? He is going around to each group of two, talking mostly to the observer. Why? Because the observer is the one who has the most important role in this teaching method. First, it's his job to observe and react in a way that enables the performer to learn the skills properly. Second, the observer learns from watching another do the tasks—hose carries in this instance—and will likely do the carries correctly when it's his turn to try it out.

Essentially, the observer becomes a teacher of sorts. How well he teaches his partner will affect how well his partner learns.

In many volunteer departments, the chief serves a two-year term. That means that every two years there will be at least one new officer in the bottom ranks. And that means new officers responsible for teaching training sessions. By teaching, while they are firefighters, how to assist someone else to learn, they will be that much more prepared when they become officers. Everyone benefits from using this teaching method.

Problem Solving

This particular teaching method has tremendous value in fire department training. In fact, many volunteers have probably been through this method but did not associate it with the term "problem solving."

Problem solving is an existing set of circumstances, conditions, or events. Certain resources are available. A solution to the problem has to be reached, given the conditions and resources available. Here is an example of how this concept can be presented to your firefighters as a case study requiring problem-solving skills.

At 11:28 a.m. on a Wednesday morning in February, the alarm goes in for a fire in a supermarket. The supermarket is located approximately 300 yards from and on a street perpendicular to a major highway. It sits in a row of commercial establishments, with at least six stores on each side of it. The supermarket itself is approximately 200 feet by 350 feet, and the roof is held together by unsupported steel truss construction.

The temperature is just below freezing, and a rain is falling, causing a layer of slick ice to form on the roadways. The first arriving unit reports heavy smoke coming from the supermarket and beginning to spread over the adjacent highway. Further investigation reveals open flame in the roof structure. The officer in charge expects the following response from his company: a total of three engines, one ladder truck, and a manpower complement of thirteen or fourteen firefighters and two officers.

What are the immediate concerns of the officer in charge? Where should he consider placement of his apparatus? What decisions should he be making?

This exercise in problem solving can be taught in a number of ways. One is for the officer to diagram the fire scene with all the information on paper and divide the training group into teams to plan a strategy. Or the training officer can diagram the fire on a blackboard and discuss it in a group session. Whatever technique he chooses to use in this class, problem solving is an excellent learning technique. It's not important that all firefighters agree on one method to fight this fire. What is important is that they are actively making decisions on fireground tactics and strategies.

Planning Training Sessions

Good training goes along with good planning. The more preparation you put into a training class, the greater the chance that it will be successful. Here are some suggestions for planning effective training sessions:

1. Decide what your objective is. Remember that an objective should be measurable, realistic, and clearly stated.
2. Plan step by step what main points you must cover in order for the volunteers to learn the skills or theories that make up the objectives. These are the building blocks of your instruction.
3. Determine what teaching methods are best for this particular training. Remember, you don't have to use one method and feel that you must stick to it through the whole lesson. Good instructors use a variety of methods during one teaching period.
4. Use demonstrations in your lesson and decide where they should be placed to help learning.
5. Remember to leave time for follow-up and review at the end of the training session. Don't assume that everyone has learned all the content. Your review reinforces what they remember and emphasizes what they might have not remembered.
6. Always allow time for questions. Don't think that everyone will fully understand and take in everything. If you don't allow time for questions, you can't clear up misunderstood ideas.

Measuring Training Effectiveness: Instructor Evaluation

If firefighters have difficulty using particular skills, even after training, it doesn't necessarily mean that they are too "dumb" to understand. It may mean that the training officer is not doing a very good job of training personnel. If this is the case, how will the officer know that he is missing the boat somewhere along the way? He can find out through instructor evaluation.

Take the time to prepare an evaluation form for officers to use. It's their way of knowing what their strong and weak points are as training officers. Certain things should be on this evaluation form. Get information on such things as:

- Were the demonstrations effective and helpful in learning the objective of the training?

- Did everyone have the opportunity to practice the skills of the training session?
- Was there time enough for both review and questions?
- Did the activities of the training follow a systematic sequence?
- Could certain parts of the training have been better held indoors or outdoors?

All these parts of effective training—performance based objectives, the classroom environment, teaching methods, planning, and evaluating—take a good deal of practice. Training abilities just don't come to someone overnight. A lot of patience and practice will, in the long run, produce effective trainings. Encourage and support these practices in your department's trainings. Let other officers know that you really endorse good teaching habits.

Beyond Departmental Training: Expanding Your Knowledge

Webster defines *ethnocentrism* as "the belief in the inherent superiority of one's own group and culture accompanied by a feeling of contempt for other groups and cultures." You don't usually hear this term around the firehouse. But when we talk about training, it has some relevance.

An ethnocentric attitude is like someone saying that "my group is the best, and we can only learn based on our own ideas and beliefs." In the fire department, you might say that officers are "ethnocentric" when they never go out of their own backyard for training. They believe that the only worthwhile training is that which they give to their firefighters. *They* know what their personnel need; any training given by someone else is a waste of time and money.

This kind of inbreeding is dangerous. It stands in the way of good fire protection planning because nothing new is ever learned. The old officers teach the new officers, and they in turn teach the firefighters. When those firefighters become officers, they pass on the same skills. Nothing new, nothing different. It's a stagnant system that perpetuates itself.

Fortunately, this situation doesn't happen as much as it used to. Growing numbers of volunteer departments are eager to go to trainings on state, regional, and national levels. This takes time and money, though. Unlike paid firefighters, volunteers cannot always take time off to attend training sessions and conferences as part of professional development. The chief, then, has a difficult job. He wants to send men to outside training and development opportunities, and yet he must be selective about which training programs are most valuable and who should attend.

My first suggestion is that company officers are the best people to attend command and leadership training programs. There is no advantage in the chief's, and in some cases the assistant chief's, being the only ones to increase their knowledge of command and leadership. Captains and lieutenants are the chiefs of tomorrow. What they can learn now will be of practical use for at least five more years.

As for other training programs, specifically technical training (e.g., hazardous materials, smoke divers school, and crash rescue), don't hesitate to select responsible firefighters. They are your officers of tomorrow. They are the ones on the front line, and whatever they can learn to make their difficult job any easier is the whole point of training. Many departments already do this.

Chiefs need to do a better job in choosing which firefighters are good choices to attend outside training programs. It should be a joint decision made by you and your officers, the ones who have the best knowledge of the firefighters under their command. Choose volunteers who have earned the privilege to go.

My second suggestion is to try, at least once a year, to get one of your officers to attend a national fire service conference. Or go yourself. I discussed the value of this early, in the public relations chapter. Despite the civilian's impression of conferences and conventions as a couple of nights on the town, some worthwhile events take place. They range from workshops and meetings to the informal but valuable get-togethers among firefighters. This chance to share ideas and experiences is where real learning gets done. And the number of topics covered in these conferences is large: training and education, fire prevention, health and fitness, emergency medical services, rural firefighting, arson, executive development, prefire planning, and the list goes on. Learning what the rest of the country is doing breaks that "ethnocentric" stranglehold.

A significant point to mention here is that volunteers often make up a large percentage of the attendees at these conferences. You will find a considerable volunteer contingent at such national conferences as those of the International Association of Fire Chiefs and Fire Department Instructors Conference, which is sponsored by the International Society of Fire Service Instructors (ISFSI). What you and your men can learn from these fire service professionals, and they can learn from you, is limitless.

Beyond Interdepartmental Training

More and more volunteer fire departments are taking advantage of skill-training opportunities outside their departments. This type of training is usually done within the state, through programs offered by the State Fire Training Director's office. But there are also highly successful technical training schools that are available to firefighters outside their states. You have to plan ahead in order to attend. Here are some suggestions:

1. Establish a master list of the major state, regional, and national fire/EMS training centers in operation. Keep on file the following information and always update it: address for application filing, fees for attendance, current schedule of courses taught, and listing of what department members have attended this particular school and courses they completed. This master list will be a valuable resource for you on training. Many people wait until it is too late to register or to have volunteers plan time off from work. You should know what schools exist and what they offer. Your inquiries will probably get you on advance mailing lists, notifying you in plenty of time to send members.

2. Maintain a specific budget for training programs. Budget not only the anticipated attendance cost but transportation expenses as well. This is going to be a difficult pill for some chiefs to swallow, considering the small budgets they have. At the same time, volunteers give enough of their time for free. If the department can cover some or all of the costs of transportation, meals, and lodging, so much the better. In any event, one facet of planning for training is budgeting for it.
3. Advance-plan well ahead of time those firefighters who will go to out-of-department training. Sometimes these programs take place on weekdays, and those who really want to attend may have to make special arrangements at their workplace weeks before they go to training.

Many outstanding training programs are held each year. To list all of them would be a lengthy task. There are, however, some notable ones that firefighters from out of state attend on a regular basis. They include the following:

Fire: Maryland Fire & Rescue Institute, University of Maryland, College Park, MD

New York State Academy of Fire Science, Montour Falls, NY

University of Illinois Fire Service Institute, Champaign, IL

Texas Fire Training Program, Texas A & M University, College Station, TX

National Fire Academy, U.S. Fire Administration, Emmitsburg, MD

California Fire Service Academy, Pacific Grove, CA

Pennsylvania State Fireman's Training School, Lewistown, PA

EMS: ACT (Acute Coronary Treatment Foundation) EMS symposiums on system design, planning, and administration.

Training and Prefire Planning

Training is most valuable when we apply it to realistic probabilities. Learning specialized skills is not an end in itself;

it is part of the overall plan to apply skills as they will be used in a specific situation.

Planning for the possible and eventual is another link in the training process. Every community has its unique fire protection problems. Where one volunteer fire department must anticipate fire-suppression action in a heavy commercial area, another will serve a rural area in which brush and forest fires are the biggest problems. Others operate in bedroom communities and must train and plan on tactics and strategies to contain fires in single-family dwellings, townhouses, and apartments.

Your responsibility is paramount in prefire planning and training. With other officers, it is your task to identify the fire-suppression hazards most prevalent in your community. If you are in a commercial area, you must know—and know well—any and all fire hazards that exist, and must have preliminary plans should fire break out.

If a major highway or busy traffic route runs through your town, a prime prefire planning target is hazardous materials transportation. Short of renting a tanker and dropping it on its side to simulate realism, you can simulate apparatus location and placement, master stream and hand line setups, traffic control, and mutual-aid response, just as if a tractor trailer had turned over and spilled hazardous volatile or toxic substances across the road.

In many instances, productive prefire planning requires close coordination with the police department, municipal leaders, and neighboring emergency services organizations. It takes lots of long-range planning for any and all circumstances that might occur, and that adds realism to the training exercise. But the dividends come when the real emergency happens, and your prefire planning/training pays off.

An example of this is when emergency service personnel stage fire and major medical incidents. This is a popular simulation exercise in which fire departments coordinate with emergency medical personnel, hospitals, police, civil defense, and other agencies and actually stage a mock disaster. It may be an airplane crash. Or the derailment of a train with subsequent fire. Or an oil refinery explosion. Whatever the circumstances, it has immense value in planning for potential emergencies and response.

Establishing Standards

Some people criticize the volunteer service for not establishing formal standards for training. Actually, this complaint is not as commonplace as it once was, for more and more departments have set down specific standards for volunteer firefighters/emergency medical technicians/paramedics to meet and maintain in order to remain active.

Nevertheless, some volunteer chiefs are trying formal standards in their department for the first time. They are not sure what standards to use. Should there be just a few classes at a county training facility?

The National Fire Protection Association has established qualifications standards that can serve to improve training standards as well. Here are the more applicable ones:

NFPA 1001: Firefighter Professional Qualifications. This standard defines three firefighter levels that set knowledge requirements in forcible entry; protective breathing apparatus; first aid; ropes; salvage; fire hose, nozzles, and appliances; fire streams; ladders; ventilation; inspection; rescue; sprinklers; fire alarm and communication; safety; fire behavior; water supplies; and overhaul and portable extinguishers. This standard has three levels of certification: Firefighter I, II, and III.

NFPA 1002: Fire Apparatus Driver/Operator Professional Qualifications. This standard covers necessary knowledge and skills in the preventive maintenance, driving, and operating of all fire department vehicles; all necessary factors in apparatus equipped with a fire pump; apparatus equipped with an aerial ladder; apparatus equipped with a tiller; and apparatus equipped with an elevating platform.

NFPA 1021: Fire Officer Professional Qualifications. This standard cites necessary knowledge categories for Fire Officer I, II, III, IV, V, and VI. Though some of the qualifications are applicable to paid departments, the majority of requirements are also applicable to volunteer officers.

Emergency Medical Technician–Ambulance (Basic Life Support) Certification. To date, there is no uniform standard for certification as an EMT-A that is acceptable in all states. In any event, the U.S. Department of Transportation, through the Emergency Medical Services Division of the National Highway Traffic Safety Administration, has established the well-known EMT-A training program. Originally 81 hours in length, this program has now been extended to approximately 105 hours. Some states have EMT certification programs that are either short of the DOT/EMT program or exceed its requirements. Check with your state's EMS division to find out the requirements your personnel have to meet.

Paramedic (Advanced Life Support) Certification. Just as with EMT-A, the EMS division of DOT has paramedic certification standards comprised of clinical, didactic, and hands-on training in excess of 400 hours. Many states have standards for paramedic certification that exceed those of DOT. The number of hours is important, but more important is the degree to which trainees get exposed to clinical practices under the supervision and direction of emergency nurses and physicians, as well as the time committed to actual training on an ambulance or mobile intensive care unit. Some leaders in the EMS field feel that in a few years, we are likely to see national standards for both basic and advanced life-support certification.

The National Fire Academy. The National Fire Academy, a division of the U.S. Fire Administration, Federal Emergency Management Agency, is not in the business of establishing standards in the fire service. Instead, its purpose is to provide a national site where fire officers can come and learn the "state of the art" in firefighting technology, organization development and management, and planning.

A goal of this national agency is that graduates of the academy, whether on-site or through field programs, will be the most likely candidates for top fire/EMS administrative positions in the years to come. The academy and Fire Administration are trying to accommodate these educational and technical training opportunities for volunteer firefighters and officers. It is hoped that future volunteer graduates of academy programs will have achieved an unwritten standard for promotion up the line.

The Bottom Line

A volunteer department may be able to lease or purchase new apparatus every five or six years. It may possess the most protective turnout gear available on the market. Its communication system may serve as a model for all emergency service providers in its region. All these benefits, however, are only as valuable as the human resources that use them.

Perhaps the bottom line is to put out the fire. After all, that's why everyone volunteered in the first place. Accomplishing that task requires precise, effective use of fire-suppression skills and abilities. Beyond that, we don't earn professional capability in management and leadership by chance. It comes to us through sound, practical training and education, as well as through experience.

In a sense, then, we must measure how good our training for the volunteer firefighter is by how well he performs on the fireground. Responsible volunteer firefighters and officers don't just happen. They learn, and when they learn well it can often be attributed to good training. Always respect this immensely important part of overall department management.

It takes time, commitment, personal energy, and perseverance to participate in designing and purchasing new fire apparatus. And you must be certain of what you're doing, to get it right the first time, and every time after that. If you don't, you can't take the truck back to the store and exchange it for another one.
—WILLIAM SICKLES, FORMER CHIEF,
MASSAPEQUA VOLUNTEER FIRE DEPARTMENT,
MASSAPEQUA, NEW YORK

10 / Selecting and Purchasing Fire Apparatus

Thirty-five members of the Smithville Volunteer Fire Department stood anxiously in front of their central firehouse, waiting to see two new engines that were due to arrive from the factory. They had waited patiently for fifteen months for this day to come. No wonder they cheered as the two gleaming red engines turned the corner and stopped in front of the apparatus bay doors. The enthusiasm was short-lived, however.

"Hey, Chief," said the president of the department, "didn't we order two rear discharges on these engines? There's only one on the back of each truck."

The chief was clearly embarrassed. "Yeah, Fred, I know. I thought that ACME fire apparatus understood what we wanted. There was a mixup somewhere."

That wasn't all. "Chief," asked another member, "I thought we were getting front steamer connections on the new engines. What happened?"

"Don't you remember? We told ACME to add them after they had already built three-quarters of the truck. It was too late for them to add the steamers."

"Well," responded the member, "maybe the new truck

committee should have told membership what they wanted to purchase in the first place. Then this wouldn't have happened."

No fire department ever accepts delivery of a new truck that doesn't have some mechanical flaws or a piece of equipment left off inadvertently at the factory. Nothing comes perfect. But the way that some departments purchase, lease, and rebuild equipment borders on a nightmare. There is no consistent planning and poor communication between the committee and the fire department members and factory representatives. No commitments are backed in writing. Misunderstandings abound. This all leads to dissatisfaction. And when you're talking about a new aerial ladder, a piece of equipment that costs close to $300,000, that is delivered with serious mechanical problems and important equipment missing, then dissatisfaction is really an understatement.

That's what this chapter is about—how to substitute old or no longer useful apparatus with newer, more useful, and more practical replacements. This chapter is not the final word, for one could write a book on specifications and apparatus purchasing. But this is a beginning point with some fundamental suggestions and information.

Maybe you're sure that you and the members in your department will buy new trucks. But you can also lease trucks and still meet your objective. Neither of these two alternatives precludes rebuilding an existing vehicle, at a cost far less than that of a new one.

Can You Justify the Need?

That sounds like a common-sense question, doesn't it? Anyone with a fair measure of intelligence shouldn't have to be reminded of it, right? Wrong!

Too many departments make a big mistake right from the start—they cannot justify the purchase of a new apparatus. Worse, they may manage to justify it, but the apparatus they want to buy (or lease) doesn't come close to matching the specific fire protection needs in the community.

Selecting and Purchasing Fire Apparatus

There's a small community, mostly farmland, located approximately ten to twelve miles south of my more densely populated and urban township. The volunteer department in this small town has a 100-foot articulating platform. Every time I see it at a parade, I keep wondering why they bought it in the first place. There isn't any building in their town that is higher than two stories. Nor have I read that any of that land is zoned for a building development in the coming years. True, it's my judgment and opinion. But I don't see a match between that platform and the building design in that community.

The greatest sham, of course, is a department that manages to buy a magnificent apparatus, not so much to fight fires with, but as a showpiece. Yes, it happens. When I attended a state training school not too long ago, I overheard one volunteer admit to another that his department did this. The fact that this occasionally happens, and that a department manages to get away with it while spending someone else's money, either contributed with best intentions or levied through taxes, is a disgrace that needs no further discussion.

I devoted a whole chapter earlier in this book to planning, and how important planning skills are to a fire officer. Whether you are a chief, a senior officer, or a company officer, you will eventually be asked to serve on an apparatus selection committee.

Planning skills apply here, too. You should set the example of encouraging your department membership to plan, well ahead of time, to replace or add fire apparatus for legitimate reasons. Three or four years of planning ahead is not unreasonable. You have to anticipate when the equipment you use now will have outlived its effectiveness.

Will you replace it now? Can it be rebuilt? Should it be? What are your sources of revenue now, and what are your financial projections three years hence, when Engine 5 will be ready for the scrapyard?

Most important, what about the master plan for your town? In the next four to five years, will your town build and complete its first high-rise buildings? Will more property be zoned for industrial and mercantile clients, thus attracting business revenues? If so, your department is going to need some functional aerial apparatus—maybe more than one piece.

I mentioned revenue. Investing your finances wisely is part of the apparatus replacement planning process. For the fire department that is an independent corporation and not subject to municipal rule, choosing, for example, to invest company finances in nothing more than the local bank's passbook savings account, which draws minimal interest, is no financial planning at all. At the time of this writing, one of the best investments around (though it has its risks) is a money market fund, which is handled by brokers from investment firms. The investor with a minimum startup figure can draw substantial interest, far more than passbook accounts yield.

I admit proudly that my own volunteer fire department has practiced sound financial investment. For the past four to five years, and under the able administrative leadership of some good presidents, we have invested money in a variety of options, including certificates of deposit, which have good rates of return. What we keep in a passbook account is small. When we needed money for two new engines, we had it.

I'm not trying to get away from the original point about planning your community's need for apparatus. But part of that planning is projecting how much equipment will cost in the years ahead, and how your fire department can invest its liquid funds in sound portfolios that will provide the needed capital to make apparatus purchases later on.

As an officer and member of the department, you can influence these issues. They are important, critically important. Know ahead of time what apparatus the department needs to replace. Know your community's fire protection needs, and select apparatus that will let you and your firefighters do the job they have to do effectively. Don't forget that it costs money to buy expensive engines and trucks; you have to plan to buy them, just as someone has to plan his or her finances for retirement.

Performance Versus Design Specifications

To discuss how to buy and select fire apparatus and not explain the difference between performance and design specifications is like having a hand line without a nozzle—you're only half prepared to do the job. Too often, selection committees order apparatus *designed* to meet many of their particular wants and desires: how large the cab should be; whether the crossbed lay of preconnected line has a universal swivel so that a firefighter can pull the same line to either side of the truck; whether the pump should be supplemented with a special cooling system so that it's less susceptible to overheating.

I'm not saying that design specifications aren't important or that a volunteer department shouldn't have the freedom to custom-order a piece of apparatus that has more features than exist on its present vehicles. But no selection committee that wants to do its job right can "spec" apparatus based solely on design features. The necessary performance specifications for the engine or aerial piece are too important, too critical, not to pay careful attention to them. Specifying the performance levels of the apparatus you want means matching as closely as possible the road conditions and fire hazards of your community with how your new apparatus will perform amid those conditions and hazards.

In 1979, Mission Research Corporation of Santa Barbara, California, prepared a five-volume document called the *Guide for Preparing Fire Pumper Apparatus Specifications*. This document takes an apparatus-selection group or department leaders step by step through the combined performance and design specifications for the department's particular fire protection and geographical conditions. Written by a project team of engineers at Mission Research that worked with a 25-member national advisory committee, the five-part guide was field-tested and validated by 11 fire departments across the United States, with successful results. The committee members who assisted with the guide represented rural and metropolitan fire department chief officers, members of fire equipment manufacturers, the National Fire Protection Association, Insurance Services Office, and various state and federal agencies including the U.S. Fire Administration and the Center for Fire Research, a unit of the National Bureau of Standards.

Lawrence M. Pietrzak and Otto A. Schleich, staff members at Mission Research, discuss the ultimate result to a fire department of following the five-part system for apparatus specifications in meshing performance and design specifications:

> The resulting specification guide stresses a performance approach, but allows design to be introduced when needed—and then with a fuller appreciation of the technical and cost implications. The resulting specification is really a hybrid, or composite, that emphasizes performance.

As described by the authors, there are certain drawbacks to design specifications. One is that concentrating on design while paying scant attention to performance and cost considerations may lead to a piece of apparatus that is underpowered, overloaded, and even unsafe. A second drawback is that an engine or truck that fails to meet needed road and pump performance criteria is unsound technically; its performance is substandard because mismatched mechanical components are used. A third drawback—one that matters in these times of high costs for goods and services—is that the more customized the design of the apparatus, the less standard it is, making it more expensive to build.

These drawbacks don't mean that design doesn't have its place. Hundreds of fire departments have proudly operated and maintained engines and trucks that were heavy on design and that have worked without serious failure in their localities. And no one can overlook the matter of personal taste in how a piece of apparatus is painted or styled.

Thus the guide—to help the purchasing department make the best choice. Following the guide's instructions through each of the five parts, you and the rest of the committee can achieve the following:

- Check or update road and pumping systems performance requirements, particularly if the road or the fire risks in the community have been changing.
- Assure that you can justify your apparatus purchase on solid cost-effective grounds.
- Assure that your specification is systematically organized and covers all important topics.
- Assure that your specification includes the most recent equipment developments, government regulations, and industry standards.

The guide, or so users are informed, is not meant to substitute for other current standards that apply to designing fire apparatus, such as SAE and the NFPA's "1901" Standard (which we'll discuss next). Neither does it take the place of government regulations, a prime one being environmental laws on gas or diesel engine emissions stipulated by the Environmental Protection Agency.

As a department committee works through the guide to find the right combination of performance and design specifications, it will do such tasks as analyze present and future fire risks in the area, examine both pumping system and other payload requirements that match local fire situations, measure road performance criteria (gradability, top speed) that correspond to some of the community's fire response route conditions and pump power requirements. After collecting much practical data, the users apply this data to some predesigned formulas that, in the end, help produce some limits of performance and design needed for any engines used in this kind of fire-protected community.

The guide has been published and can be purchased by contacting the Superintendent of Documents, U.S. Government Printing Office, Washington, D.C. 20402. All purchasers must enclose either a check or a money order with order. When ordering materials, specify the identifying titles, numbers, and codes of each part as listed here:

Part I. Executive Summary
GPO 064-000-000-11-0 ($1.75)

Part II. Determining Performance Requirements
GPO 064-000-000-12-8 ($5.50)
Part III. Preparing the Bid Specification
GPO 064-000-000-13-6 ($8.00)
Part IV. A Suggested Specification Format
GPO 064-000-000-14-4 ($4.75)
Part V. Supplementary Material
GPO 064-000-000-15-2 ($5.50)

Where to Start?

Whether the choice is to buy now or lease now, the department still needs some guidelines, some mapped-out course of action to follow, which will ultimately end with a new engine or truck that is, if not exactly what the customer ordered, close to it. There are several ways to get guidelines. One choice is to consult other local departments, asking the officers and truck committee members how they prepared the specifications for their most recent purchases. Another choice is to contact some of the reputable apparatus manufacturers directly—Mack, Pierce, Hahn, American LaFrance, Emergency One, Seagrave, Sutphen, LTI, Gruman, and others—and request material that the company provides to fire departments planning to write apparatus specifications. These companies are glad to help. The better you can prepare specifications that they can understand (and most manufacturers probably make the same suggestions to all spec writers), the easier their job will be in giving your department the kind of bid it is looking for.

Remember, putting a bid together is time-consuming. And it costs money to do it. The manufacturer doesn't pay staff members to write specifications for free. The bidder, regardless of the company, wants its bid to be the best that it can produce. The company honestly wants to do business with you.

Another way to obtain guidelines is to write for specifications that support the guidelines presented in the *National Fire Protection Association's Standard No. 1901, Automotive Fire Apparatus, 1979.* At times, borrowing the format of another department's specifications may be some help, but it is no guarantee of success. The other department may have been disappointed with the apparatus they bought, a fact they may not be ready to admit to you or to anyone else. Moreover, a lot of the specs may not be suited to your needs.

The *1901 Standard* covers specifications for all varieties of engines and aerial apparatus. It describes provisions they apply to apparatus equipped with a fire pump, hose body, booster pump, water tank, aerial ladder, elevating platform, and water tower. There are also two chapters that cover equipment for different kinds of apparatus as well as what acceptance tests new apparatus must pass successfully in order to be considered acceptable for emergency service.

The Appendix to the *Standard* supplies some important information, too, ranging from a "Study of Apparatus Needs," and "Compliance with Federal Standards" to "Writing the Specifications" and "Awarding the Contract." The two most salient statements in the *Standard* appear in the beginning of the text. First, under the section titled "Purpose," it is stated that the requirements for fire apparatus described are minimum requirements only. They are offered to serve you and your fellow committee members as a solid, practical starting point. You can use them to prepare the technical specifications for the apparatus you want. Second, the "Application" section states that the individual purchaser should apply the text's basic performance standards to his particular fire protection needs and how the apparatus will be used and operated. In this respect it is consistent with the *Guide for Preparing Fire Pumper Apparatus Specifications*.

Buying New

Few things are more eventful for a volunteer than the day that new apparatus arrives. It is a moment of which to be proud. In addition, you realize that you and your men will depend on that vehicle to operate effectively through the toughest conditions. Most of the time, you'll depend on the performance of that vehicle for your safety.

Buying a new piece of apparatus, from the moment the department comes up with the idea to the day it arrives, is a time-consuming job. It takes long hours and lots of planning and replanning. There are many meetings and discussions, sometimes with differences of opinion. It means dealing with manufacturers. The experience, tough as it is, need not be full of troubles. If you and the committee start off properly, the whole process can be smooth and systematic.

Here are suggestions for a systematic approach. This is not the one and only way to do it; I am not suggesting that. But after reviewing and researching this aspect of department management, I found these ideas to be almost universal.

Define and Justify Need

I know I just discussed this, but don't forget it. It's the most important thing to remember.

Picking the Apparatus Selection Committee

If you are a chief or a senior officer, you are probably a committee member, if not the committee chairman. If you are a junior officer, you're likely to be appointed and can suggest what other members, based on their knowledge and skill, should serve with you. The number of members is not that important; it's insignificant whether the committee has four members or ten members. What does matter is that responsible persons serve on the committee, people who can make it work.

Let's assume that as an officer in the department, other than chief, you have been asked to select the remaining members of the committee. Whom do you choose?

First, find a writer, someone who can put words on paper clearly and understandably. Use him to write the specifications, both performance and design. Also use him to write correspondence between the department and the bidding companies, or the Board of Fire Commissioners and municipal officials. I cannot impress on you enough how important it is to have a skilled writer on the committee. If you don't have such a writer, maybe one of the commiteemen's wives can do this job for you, on a limited basis and at her convenience.

Next, find a member who knows how to negotiate business contracts and handle purchase orders and agreements. Not every department has such a person, someone whose day-to-day work includes writing proposals and purchase agreements for large sums of money, and sitting down at a table with other parties to negotiate a suitable purchase agreement for everyone. If you have such a member, you're lucky. Use him for his fine abilities. This person's knowledge is invaluable when you are purchasing new apparatus. He can distinguish good bids from questionable or unclear ones, and can advise the committee on what to concede and what to hold out for when they negotiate with bidding manufacturers.

Select a member who knows a lot about the apparatus currently available on the market. I'm talking about someone who knows more than the difference between an aerial scope and a tower ladder. He should be someone who can advise you and the committee, officers, and membership on varieties of engines (automotive), transmissions, cab designs, chassis designs, and other factors. If you lack someone in the department who has this knowledge about apparatus, then select a responsible member who can research all that you need to know. The information he comes up with will make things easier for the committee when it is ready to write its performance and design specifications.

Some people suggest that an officer from the engine company that will receive the new vehicle be a member of the committee. This idea has its risks. If the fire department is set up so that a member responds only to the company to which he is assigned, then the members of that company are the ones who will use the apparatus almost exclusively. But this arrangement is usually the exception instead of the rule. Most department SOPs state that a member will respond to the firehouse closest to where he is when the alarm goes in. If, for instance, I respond from my house, then I always go to the same firehouse where my gear is hanging, Station 1. But if I'm out shopping on Saturday and happen to be a few blocks away from Station 2 when a call comes over my radio, then I'm expected to respond there.

What I'm leading up to is that some members may feel that having this company officer on the committee is unethical. Some may claim that the officer will support purchasing certain features on the new vehicle because his crew will use it most. But their argument is that all members of the department will use the new engine or truck, not just the men in Company 4. Does this sound like a petty issue? Maybe it is. But does it happen? Absolutely.

I witnessed a related incident recently when a department ordered two new engines. The new vehicles were assigned to two of three firehouses, the two satellite stations. In no time at all, some members charged the chief with bias judgment; they claimed that he had placed one of the two new engines at his old company station instead of the main stationhouse. The arguments persisted for at least three months, with everyone being territorial and quickly forgetting that each of them was a member of the same fire department, regardless of which station he responded to. And the chief wasn't even a member of the apparatus selection committee!

My advice is to staff the committee with persons whose skills and knowledge are a must—the writer, the negotiator and buyer, and the information researcher. Fill the rest of the committee seats with members who have strong reputations for their honesty, wisdom, reasoning, and most of all, their impartiality. Don't have any committee members who someone may even *suspect* of having ulterior motives.

Selecting the Basics

Now that you have your justification to buy or lease, and have a committee to work with, decide what fundamental features you want on your new vehicle. Some of the features to consider are these:

- Gas vs. diesel engine
- Standard or automatic transmission
- Pump size and pumping capacity
- Front-mounted vs. rear-mounted aerial ladder
- Size and weight of the vehicle
- Types of portable ladders to attach
- Location of all hose beds
- Types and diameter of hose

You can make these *tentative* decisions in several ways. One is to assess what features your present vehicles have and do not have. Then ask yourself what you don't have on your present apparatus that you feel you need. Remember, you haven't necessarily analyzed all your performance specifications yet. Still, you have some ideas on the basic features that will give you the engine or aerial piece you need for fire protection in your area.

Another way is to consult with some neighboring fire departments whose protection areas are similar to yours. How has their apparatus met or failed to meet their needs? How do they like the automatic diesel engine they bought almost two years ago? Do they have any trouble getting their tower ladder around street corners?

I realize that this suggestion sounds like common sense. Well, maybe so. But that doesn't mean that everyone practices common sense, or that a prospective purchasing department will have the practical sense to look close to its own backyard to find some important information.

Whatever you do to come up with your draft ideas for basic specifications, don't forget that they should be tentative. Nothing says that you must cast them in bronze the first time.

WRITE YOUR FIRST DRAFT OF SPECIFICATIONS

This is the time to go to the sources such as the *1901 Standard* and the *Guide* to verify both the performance and design specifications you need. After you finish your thorough analysis, match the results to the earlier basic features you identified. Keep those features that will meet your needs. Throw out those that are impractical for your department. You might learn that you don't, in fact, need to custom-order a new engine but that you can get one on a commercial chassis that will perform magnificently for you, saving money at the same time.

Adding Up the Frills

It's common sense to try to buy the apparatus you want at the best price you can get. But you won't get everybody to agree how to price-out your final choice of cab, pump, chassis, and other features. You can get some immediate help by following the performance guidelines we discussed earlier. Once you are sure of your performance and design needs, though, I suggest that you add on all the frills you *think* you can afford; special generator housings in the compartments, extra discharge gates, aesthetic features in the cab, aluminum wheels, painting and striping; the list goes on.

These add up to be expensive items. But any purchase is also a negotiation, and everything is negotiable. With some manufacturers, you may have to forego several features because you decide that you want to buy from a particular manufacturer, even if his price is higher than that of some other bidders. On the other hand, you may negotiate many of your desired features and get a price that you can afford. You've lost nothing by trying.

Before you present your membership with suggestions for performance and design specifications, look over your present vehicles. Whatever they lack that you want, add it to your list. You can always drop some items later.

Presenting your Draft Specifications

An account executive in advertising can work for weeks or months to put together ideas for his client's new campaign. The ideas are only as good as the creative mind in which they originated. But the account executive will admit that the make-break point in his business is the formal presentation to the client. If the president of a major airline likes the campaign proposal presented to him, it can mean a multimillion-dollar account for the agency. If the presentation is weak—poorly prepared, poor-quality audiovisuals, all materials not available—then the best creative minds in the business won't be able to keep the airline president from taking his business to another agency.

You and the rest of the committee face the same challenges as that account executive. If you want to sell your specifications ideas to membership, the Board of Fire Commissioners, or municipal officials, you must prepare a professional presentation. How do you do it?

1. Pick a committee member who speaks clearly and is comfortable in front of groups. He should make the official presentation. A poor presenter can ruin a presentation.
2. Write out a detailed outline of what information you will present. From this outline, prepare a one-page fact sheet of major discussion points and pass it out to all those present at the committee's presentation. Don't pass out your original plan because the audience members will spend time reading what you handed out to them instead of listening to the presentation.
3. Prepare any charts or graphs that illustrate the reasons for your recommendations: price figures, differences in standard features, choices in chassis designs, and so on. Design and write these visual aids clearly on a chalkboard or a flip chart so that everyone in the audience can see them.
4. Make photocopies of any pictures of apparatus choices you propose to buy. Let people see what you're considering. After all, it will be their apparatus too.
5. Explain clearly what work the committee has done, and what it proposes to do next, pending the approval and go-ahead of the governing body.
6. Allow time for a question-and-answer period. If you are the presenter and you expect some questions to which you might not

know the answers, make sure you have someone from the committee who can answer questions. Be ready to finish the presentation with as few issues remaining as possible. And if you don't know the answer to something, make sure that you get it.
7. Set a time limit on the presentation. Confine it to the most essential information. The audience will appreciate this consideration; you'll keep their attention longer, and you will appear more sure of your mission and what you propose to do next.
8. Let the membership or fire commissioners know when you'll be meeting them next to give them a progress report. And let them know that you will call a meeting if any unusual circumstances come up that must be resolved immediately.

Writing the Final Specifications

After you get membership approval, hire a professional typist to type the complete final specifications that you will then send to all potential bidders. Once you have the final typed copy, have extra sets reproduced at a printing shop on a finely finished photocopy. Finally, attach a cover letter to each bidder, and have the letter's author, usually the committee chairman, sign each letter personally.

It's simple. A bidder who reads a polished, professionally written set of specifications will take you seriously. And if you put together a sloppy set of specs, you'll likely find some reputable manufacturers who choose not to bid at all. They'll assume that your sloppy work is a measure of how your department does business. Remember, a well-produced product carries credibility.

The Evaluation Form

Prepare a detailed evaluation form before you send out specifications to bidders. This is a must. How are you going to compare one bidder with another? Will you rate the desired parts of each bid by a numerical ranking? Will you differentiate between desired features and required features on the bidder's specifications? Do bids need to meet a minimum score before the number you're considering is narrowed down? And will you eliminate bidders immediately because of cost?

Don't neglect your evaluation form. You cannot expect to make a sound, practical, and possibly legally unbiased decision if you don't have some systematic method for rating choices.

If one bidder feels that his company wasn't given a fair evaluation, you certainly better be ready to prove that his bid specifications were evaluated fairly and objectively against all the others. Fail to do that, and you could bring considerable headaches to yourself and your department. (A later part of this chapter presents an evaluation model.)

GET AN OUTSIDE OPINION

After all this time and work, you're probably pleased with how your specifications look. You've made every effort to be thorough and exacting. But don't send the specs out yet. Instead, give a set to someone you know who is not associated with the fire department. Select a person you respect as a tough critic, a person with a questioning mind.

Though this person is not in the fire service, and doesn't understand the language of the profession, he or she should still be able to read your specs and understand what you want to build. It should be clear from reading the specifications just what you want and how you want it.

You should then rewrite any part of your specs that the reviewer finds unclear or confusing. If he or she doesn't understand what you mean, it's possible that the manufacturer may also misunderstand. You don't need any misunderstandings, not when you're paying out a few hundred thousand dollars. You want *every* part of those specs to be clear.

SENDING AND RECEIVING BIDS

It's the committee's choice as to how many manufacturers they wish to receive bids. Why narrow your choices? After all the work, all you're putting forth now is the cost of postage to send out the specifications. Unless you know one manufacturer that you absolutely do not want to do business with, send specs to anyone who might build your vehicle for you.

Now, some legal common-sense advice. Check on all local, regional, and state laws concerning the competitive bid process among manufacturers. And abide by the law!

An incorporated department that supports itself financially through donations and doesn't answer to any governing municipal group can be more subjective in choosing and evaluating bidders. But that is certainly not the case for municipally controlled departments or fire districts. It's likely that laws govern equipment and materials purchases made through the competitive bid process. Learn what they are, and what you must do, *before* you send out bids. Consult your department lawyer if you aren't sure how to interpret such laws.

State specifically in your cover letter to manufacturers how you want their bids to be prepared and submitted, when the bids are due or should be postmarked, and that each will be treated as a sealed bid. Also state when bids will be opened, the last date they will be evaluated, and the latest date that bidders will learn whether their submitted specifications are or are not under consideration.

Evaluating Bids

Choosing an acceptable bid need not be difficult if you follow an organized method of rating each manufacturer's bids against your criteria. Figure 10.1 shows a suggested format to evaluate bids. Though there are several widely known management consulting firms that present similar formats when they hold seminars on decision-making skills in the business world, concepts here follow a decision-making process designed by Charles H. Kepner and Benjamin B. Tregoe, two famous management development specialists. What I like most about this evaluation form is that it works especially well when you have to decide from among several choices. Here's how to use it:

REQUIRED FEATURES	Name of Bidder:			Name of Bidder:			Name of Bidder:			Name of Bidder:		
	Data	Yes/No		Data	Yes/No		Data	Yes/No		Data	Yes/No	
DESIRED FEATURES	**Value**											
		Data	S	T	Data	S	T	Data	S	T	Data	S
FINAL TOTAL SCORE ____		FINAL TOTAL SCORE ____			FINAL TOTAL SCORE ____			FINAL TOTAL SCORE ____			FINAL TOTAL SCORE ____	

Figure 10.1. Apparatus Bid Evaluation Form.
S = Score; T = Total Award for Feature.

1. In the box at the top far left of the sheet, list all *required* features. "Required" means those features that you insist on having and will not compromise on, such as a certain diesel engine size.
2. Now with one bidder being Alternative A, and the next Alternative B, and so on, mark yes or no as to whether each bidder does or does not meet each of your requirements. When you're done, every bidder that offers all your requirements is still acceptable; those that don't are eliminated.

    I repeat: If everything is not clear as you read a bidder's specifications proposal, call or write and ask for clarification. Once you have it, then evaluate.
3. Next, list in the lower far left column all the *desired* features you would want on the apparatus; items you would like to have but that are not necessary.
4. Give each desired feature some measurable value: For example, on a 1 to 10 scale, a desired feature that you really want on your vehicle would have a high value for you, possibly 10. Another feature might be nice yet insignificant, so its value is estimated at 2. Two features can have the same value.
5. Now rate how well or poorly each bidder's specifications can provide each desired feature you want. Then multiply the desired feature's value times the score the bidder earned for that feature. *Example:* Our committee feels that having extra deep compartments in the rear is semi-important; we rate its value as 7. Bidder A can do this for us and not lose too much space in the hose bed. We thus rate that manufacturer's ability to do this as 8. Final score for that desired feature times its value = 56.

    You must follow this procedure for each desired feature and for every bidder. Total up all the point scores for each bidder. The one with the highest point total should be your choice for the contract award. *Point of Information:* Using numbers is simply one way for ranking bidders. Some choose to use a system of plus (+), minus (−), and zero (0). The bidder with the most pluses, or the least minuses, is the best choice. The decision on what measurable system to use is arbitrary.

Don't feel that you are bound by this method of evaluation or that you must choose the bidder who comes out on top. No matter how good the method, people cannot help but be somewhat subjective when they make decisions. Though both in the acceptable price range, for example, a bid from Mack and another from American LaFrance may be awfully close in total score. Mack has the highest point total, but you choose the other. Why? Because your department would like to add a LaFrance, even though both vehicles cost about the same, and Mack looks a little better overall. The final decision factor was that American LaFrance is closer to you, and service might be easier.

An important warning: Be honest with all bidders. If you say that this is an open competition, be true to your word. Don't lead some bidders on, and all the time know that you plan to choose a specific manufacturer. This isn't misleading, it's dishonest. And if you falsify your real intentions, you may be challenged in court by one of the losing bidders.

If you want Pierce to build your department an engine, then don't waste any other manufacturer's time asking for specifications; simply tell Pierce to build what you want and pay for it. Any bad business practices you participate in will blemish your department's reputation for a long time to come. It's a large price to pay for a quick indiscretion.

Meeting the Manufacturer's Representatives

Let's say that, after reviewing and evaluating nine different bids, you come up with three that are close. Instead of feeling forced to select one bid, discuss among the committee members a personal meeting with representatives of the final bidders. The representatives will likely come to see you, at your convenience and at your firehouse, so that you don't have to go to any great trouble or expense. You'll be glad that you did this.

The representative may suggest that you change your specification wording as it covers a particular feature of the apparatus. Don't ever exclude the judgment of the manufacturers. That's their business, and most of them know it well. He might also forewarn you that all future models of his company's apparatus will not carry a particular major feature after next year. If you want to purchase more of his company's vehicles, and you like that feature, don't overlook this information. Any reputable representative will want you to see some of his company's work that other departments nearby use. Those engines and trucks represent his company's work, and he wants to show it off.

Making the Final Choice

After all the correspondence, meetings, evaluations, follow-up meetings, and remaining discussions, the committee has to make its decision. The points here are brief. Stay consistent with the conditions you stated in the original cover letter to manufacturers. Don't hesitate in notifying losing bidders. Send each one a letter thanking the company for its time and effort in putting together a fine specification bid. And, finally, arrange a meeting with the winning manufacturer's representative and verify in writing all that the company will do as it builds your vehicle.

Pitfalls

There are some large holes you might fall into when you decide to purchase apparatus. Stay out of these holes, and avoid the following pitfalls:

1. Avoid vague specifications. Don't assume that a bidding manufacturer will necessarily understand what you want. Make sure that all terminology you use means the same thing to the other party reading it.
2. Stay away from brand names whenever possible. The only exception to this is engines, transmissions, and pumps. Otherwise, state in your specifications for the feature to be "made by Acme hose reels or equal in quality to."
3. The closer you can select a manufacturer who is close to your

Selecting and Purchasing Fire Apparatus

department geographically, the better off you may be. In fact, you may make location where the engine or truck will be built a desired feature.

4. Don't necessarily take the salesman at his word. He may be truthful in what he is telling you, yet may not know something that company officials do. Get everything confirmed in writing *and on the manufacturer's stationery.*
5. Make sure that your specifications become a part of the contract documents. Have everyone involved initial it as such.
6. Make certain that your specifications make it to the factory shop. Confirm receipt of these documents through registered mail. Specs can be taken off important papers before they reach the shop.
7. Stay on the manufacturer's back so that they maintain production schedules. Don't ask for delayed deliveries. You might not foresee some eventuality such as a strike that can really set your delivery date back.
8. Be explicit in your testing requirements. Ask for testing results that are *certified in accordance with Underwriter's Laboratories.* Don't settle for testing requirements to be checked by any sister companies of the manufacturer. Insist that testing procedures comply with NFPA Standard 1901.
9. Schedule two visits to the factory. More important, leave the second visit for just before the trucks leave the factory and are put on the road. When they call you and say that the vehicle(s) is ready, tell them to wait, then get out there as quickly as you can. A lot of departments have been stung by not making this last-minute visit.
10. Let the manufacturer deliver the vehicle to you. Don't offer to pick it up and drive back. If problems occur, let them be the responsibility of the manufacturer.
11. Get transportation charges and expenses included in the total price of the contract. This means the two visits by members of your committee to the factory. Don't let the manufacturer talk you into adding this part as a clause to the contract. If money is tight, you might cut out the trips and live to regret it.
12. Make sure that your cover letter to manufacturers explains without any misunderstanding just what you expect them to comply with when they draw up specifications for you.

13. *Always* have an abbreviated acceptance test right after delivery of the vehicle and in the presence of both the salesman and the delivery engineer. If you are to have any problems, you definitely want them there to see them. Otherwise, they may not accept your word for it.
14. Put the burden on the manufacturer to abide by the particular state and federal laws to which the vehicle's building and operation must comply.
15. Specify that the apparatus will be built for fire service use and not just commercial use. The difference will be obvious to you years later when your vehicle is still operating.
16. Know how many years you plan to use this apparatus; this will affect all the specifications you seek and what you look for in a new engine or truck.
17. Try to keep your specifications to as basic or standard a vehicle as you can. Custom work can be costly. The closer you can get to what they build off the line, the better off you will be. This is where it's important to talk face to face with the manufacturer's representative to get his opinions.
18. Keep an open mind. Take and consider the manufacturer's suggestions. Don't be stubborn or unyielding in what you want and don't want on the vehicle.

Leasing as an Option

In 1975, fire service leaders in Prince Georges County, Maryland, a densely populated suburb of Washington, D.C., with over twenty volunteer fire departments in which volunteers serve with career firefighters from the county's fire and rescue service, faced a serious problem. They needed to purchase some new and critically needed fire apparatus immediately.

Prince Georges Chief Jim Estepp had several obstacles with which to contend. The county's budget did not contain enough surplus money to purchase two new engines and ladder trucks. It didn't look like the county would have any money in the near future for such a purchase. It also seemed highly improbable to float a bond issue before the taxpayers, an act that would have plunged the county's budget into the red. And bonding companies didn't want to handle bonds, spanning a 15-year period, to cover fire apparatus that could easily be damaged or rendered inoperable long before the vehicles were paid off.

The Volunteer Fire Commission in Prince Georges County, which oversees budgets for the volunteer departments, asked Estepp and the county executive to find out whether leasing new apparatus was a viable alternative to the problem.

In this particular instance, the answer was definitely yes. By contacting a number of apparatus manufacturers, Estepp and the county Volunteer Fire Commission learned that some apparatus firms would lease apparatus to them for a five-year period. At the end of the five years, the county would pay off the balance and own the vehicles. The lease agreement also allowed the county the option of ending the lease at any time by paying whatever balance remained on the original purchase price.

The result? In late 1976, after preparing specifications and accepting and evaluating bids, the county took possession of two new engines, two 100-foot rear mount aerial ladders, and six ambulances, all built by reputable manufacturers. One year later, sixteen more ambulances were placed in service throughout the county's fire stations, and in the same year, 1977, the county government approved a short-term note to pay for the leased apparatus. Said Estepp, as he reflected on this experience, "The lease-purchase method of acquiring apparatus might not be everyone's cup of tea, but for those with an immediate need for equipment and a short-term shortage of ways to pay for it, it certainly is worth reviewing.

Estepp is right when he suggests that leasing might not necessarily be the best way for a department to procure new apparatus. Leasing, you'll find, is like anything else; it has its good points and its problems. That's why your committee, if considering leasing as an alternative, should research the idea thoroughly. What, then, are some of the advantages and problems?

On the plus side, you might discover a leasing agreement (depending on the leasing institution) that includes maintenance on the apparatus, much the same as exists with some automobile-leasing operations. While the department leases an engine or truck, the leasor is responsible for maintaining the apparatus through regular interval checks on everything from the air pressure system to the power takeoff, to see that it is constantly operating safely and effectively. Even if maintenance is not included in the central agreement, it can sometimes be purchased as an added feature. You'll have to check out how much that will cost.

A second advantage of leasing is that it gets around the problem of a bond purchase, though voter approved, that has little probability of success because interest rates are too high or because the locality isn't in a position to be borrowing money.

A third advantage is that you can invest whatever liquid capital the fire department has in sound financial investments where the rate of return surpasses the interest penalty you have to pay on the loan for the vehicle. For example, your department may decide to lease a new pumper. The cost is $100,000, and the lease will be spread out over five years, at an interest penalty of 15 percent on the lease. The leasing company, of course, turns over a check for the total purchase amount to the manufacturer. In the meantime, your department invests its money in some venture that earns greater interest than 15 percent, such as the money market funds I mentioned earlier. At the time of this writing, some money market funds are drawing as much as 17.8 percent. And the interest is compounded daily. Or you might take part of your assets and purchase a Treasury note that is yielding a rate of interest that is equal to or more than 15 percent.

I couldn't discuss this aspect of financing without presenting one valuable piece of information. It is highly probable that, as you are reading this book, federal law will allow volunteer fire departments existing as nonprofit organizations to accept loans with which to purchase or make capital investments *with-*

out having to pay any interest obligation that accompanies the loan. If this is so, it makes the option of leasing even more attractive.

You should, without question, know about financial options that can bring in considerable amounts of money. I cannot imagine any progressive volunteer fire department not having some member who knows and understands the workings of Wall Street, a member who can advise membership of the advantages and disadvantages of everything from blue chip stocks and municipal bonds to gold and corporation and utility bonds.

Finally, an obvious advantage is that, when you lease, you can spread out the payments of your purchase. You get the vehicle you need without paying everything out in one lump sum.

Now for some of the pitfalls. There are two of which I will warn you. First, make sure the lease agreement is not one that has add-on interest. Add-on interest means that you're paying interest on the equal yearly amounts of the total purchase price instead of the balance. Let's take, for instance, the same $100,000 pumper leased for five years. If the interest rate were 10 percent, then an add-on system would make you pay $10,000 interest each of the five years, instead of 10 percent of the continuing balance, which will be reduced in principal with each payment.

What you want in your agreement is simple interest, just paying interest on the balance. So, after the first year, if you have paid back $20,000 toward the principal sum, then you would begin the second year by paying only 10 percent on $80,000, and that figure of course would itself diminish each month as payments were made.

The second pitfall is having to pay a penalty fee for paying off the loan balance. You should, without a doubt, try to get a lease-purchase agreement that allows your department to pay off the principal balance any time before the lease expires, *without penalty.*

Not all the fire apparatus manufacturers have lease programs, nor do the ones that do all have standard agreements. Mack Trucks, for example, does not have a lease-purchase program through its national office in Allentown, Pennsylvania. The fire apparatus division, however, is at present conducting a survey to see how prevalent as well as popular leasing is, and whether it might be a means of purchasing equipment from their company in the future. Yet some of Mack's regional centers may have their own lease plans or can recommend commercial lease companies with which to deal.

American LaFrance does have a lease program. Handled through A-T-O Leasing, the lease corporation for the company (American LaFrance is a subsidiary of A-T-O, Inc.), leases can be obtained for as little as three years and as long as seven years. The program is a simple interest plan, and at the end of the lease period, the fire department purchases the vehicle for a sum of one dollar, taking title to the vehicle.

Some final words. Leasing can certainly be a suitable apparatus purchase option. Know its advantages and pitfalls. Study lease contracts carefully, taking them to your lawyer if necessary. Contact all manufacturers to find out if they offer lease-purchase plans and how they work. Know exactly what you're doing before you sign on the dotted line.

And Finally, Rebuilding

Rebuilding fire apparatus is not a new idea. Many departments have done it before, either restoring a failing vehicle so that it is once again ready to use as a first or second line unit or redesigning it so that it serves various functions, such as a combined rescue and first attack unit.

But volunteer fire department leaders now consider rebuilding just as viable an option as purchasing new from the factory. Why? Economics. Money is tight, interest rates are high, and new apparatus is awfully expensive. Why not think about rebuilding your 1971 aerial ladder at a cost one-half the amount that the department would pay for a new one?

As with leasing, there are no standard specifications that apparatus manufacturers endorse or sponsor for rebuilding.

Selecting and Purchasing Fire Apparatus ◀ 217

Guidelines differ with the manufacturer, and not all manufacturers, at least at this time, even rebuild apparatus. Once again, you and the other committee members must do your homework.

If, in fact, you decide that rebuilding is your best temporary option and that you want to postpone buying a new truck for at least four years, then most of the same suggestions I discussed about bidding procedures with new apparatus apply. Even if you don't go to bid, but decide that you want a particular manufacturer to rebuild your vehicle, awarding a contract directly, you should still follow practical, common-sense guidelines, especially the pitfalls of the purchasing process.

For example, wouldn't you want to visit the factory just before the rebuilt vehicle is delivered, just as you would do if you had it built from scratch? How about testing? Wouldn't you insist that the rebuilding company test the vehicle according to Underwriter's Laboratories performance standards, and not test it by a sister company of the manufacturer? You're using the same methods. Only the means of obtaining a new or more useful piece of apparatus has changed.

Explore rebuilding as an alternative. Consult all the manufacturers, and find out who rebuilds or restores apparatus. Meet with company representatives, and get all your questions asked before you sign your name on the contract.

As I said in the beginning of this chapter, the subject of selecting and purchasing new fire apparatus is so detailed that an entire book could be written about it. My purpose has been to get you started, to give you some fundamental information that will make this time-consuming, energy-sapping venture more successful, and I hope, less painful than it often is.

Index

A-B-C-D method of writing performance-based objectives, 173
Accidents, 159–60
Accountability, 147–48
Action planning, 38–42
Aerobic fitness, 144
American LaFrance, 216
Apparatus, selecting and purchasing, 189–217
   basic features wanted in new vehicle, 200–1
   bids, evaluation of, 206, 208–9
   bids, sending and receiving, 205–6
   evaluation form, 204–5
   final choice, making the, 210
   first draft of specifications, 201–2
   frills, 202
   guidelines for, 196–97
   justifying the purchase of new apparatus, 190–92
   leasing as an alternative to, 211–16
   manufacturer's representatives, meeting with, 209–10
   new apparatus, 197–210
   NFPA's Standard No. 1901, 196–97
   outside opinions on, 205
   performance and design specifications, 193–96, 201–4
   pitfalls in, 210–12
   planning, 191–92
   presenting your draft specifications, 202–4
   rebuilding apparatus as alternative to, 216–17
   writing the final specifications, 204
Apparatus selection committee, 198–200
Applicants
   discrimination against, 155–56
   health and fitness of, 140–41
   medical-physical assessment of, 141–45

personality types of, 148–51
See also Membership application; Recruitment of members
A-T-O Leasing, 216
Awards, 125–28

Blake, Robert R., 12, 18, 20
Blanchard, Kenneth H., 22, 24
Blood chemistry workup, 154
Blood pressure
 cardiovascular disease and, 142, 154
 screening program, 70
Bids for new apparatus
 evaluating, 206, 208–9
 sending and receiving, 205–6
Board of Fire Commissioners, 80–82
Budgeting, 85–96
 for training programs, 184
Business meetings, 55

Cardio-pulmonary resuscitation (CPR) training, 69–70
Cardiovascular disease, 140–43
 legal issues, 153–55
Chain of command, 117–19
Cholesterol, cardiovascular disease and, 142
Classroom setting for training, 173–75
Committee action plan, 39–40
Communication
 emergency driving and, 161–62
 feedback and, 122–24
 listening and, 120
 open-door policy and, 119–21
Community, educating the, 62–66, 71

Community events, public relations and, 53–54, 68–71
Completion dates for performance objectives, 34–35
Conferences, professional, 62, 182–83

Davis, Paul O., 143–44
Death of firefighters, 160
Delegation of responsibilities, 33–34
Design specifications, 193–96, 201–4
Disciplinary charges, 162–63
Discrimination, 155–56
Dismissal of members, 162–64
Doctor, fire department, 143
Driving, emergency, 160–62

Emergency driving, 160–62
Emergency Medical Technician-Ambulance (Basic Life Support) certification, 187
Employment history in membership application, 136–37
Employment record of applicants, 132
Estepp, Jim, 212
Ethnocentric attitudes, 181
Evaluation forms, 204
Exercise, cardiovascular disease and, 143

Financial management, 76-96
 incorporated independent departments, 77–79

Index

part paid/part volunteer departments, 83-85
volunteer fire districts, 79-82
See also Budgeting
Fire apparatus. *See* Apparatus, selecting and purchasing
Fire chiefs associations, meetings of, 54-55
Fire Commissioners, Board of, 80-82
Fire districts, 79-82
Fireground command simulation, fireground officer selection and, 107-111
Fireground officer selection, 96-114
criteria for, 100-11
modifying the fire department constitutional process, 99
NFPA No. 1021: Fire Officer Professional Qualifications, 111-13
oral examination and, 102-7
personnel record and, 100-1
popularity and, 97-99
selection board, 99-100, 113-14
written examination and, 101-2
Fire incident reports, 164-66
Fire prevention program, 35-36
Fire prevention seminars, 71
Fire protection areas, 166-67
Force Field Analysis, 44-47
Fund drives, 51-53

Goals
objectives distinguished from, 171-73
See also Planning

Greensburg, Pennsylvania, Volunteer Fire Department, 141
Grid model. *See* Managerial grid
Guide for Preparing Fire Pumper Apparatus Specifications, 193-95, 197

Heart attacks, 140
legal issues, 153-55
See also Cardiovascular disease
Heart disease. *See* Cardiovascular disease
Hersey, Paul, 22, 24
Hypertension, 70, 142, 154

Independent departments, 77-79
Injuries, 159-60

Kepner, Charles, H., 206

Leadership styles, 11-31
counterproductive, 29-30
"everybody's buddy" officers, 29-30
grid model of, *see* Managerial Grid
"know-it-all" officers, 29
"panic button" officers, 30
participatory management, 30-31
Situational Leadership theory of, *see* Situational Leadership theory
Learn Not to Burn fire prevention curriculum, 35
Leasing fire apparatus, 212-16

Lectures, 176–77
Legal issues, 152–67
  applicant discrimination, 155–56
  disciplinary charges and dismissal, 162–64
  emergency driving, 160–62
  fire incident reports, 164–66
  fire protection areas, 166–67
  injuries and medical evaluation, 159–60
  physical requirements and standards, 153–55
  training and certification standards, 157–59
Library, 158
Line officers. *See* Fireground officer selection
Listening, 120
Local government, relations between fire department and, 50–56

Mack Trucks, 215–16
Magazines, fire service, 61, 158
Managerial Grid, 12–22
  1,1-oriented fire officer, 14, 16
  1,9-oriented fire officer, 12, 15–16
  5,5-oriented fire officer, 14, 16
  9,1-oriented fire officer, 12–15
  9,9-oriented fire officer, 16–18
  new version of, 18–20
  realistic approach to, 20–21
Maturity of applicants, 132
Media, relations with, 57–61
Medical-physical assessment, 141–45
Membership. *See* Applicants; Recruitment of members

Membership applications, 133, 135–40
  applicant's written portion, 137
  employment history in, 136–37
  general data in, 136
  nondiscriminatory, 155–56
  nonfire responsibilities, section on, 138
  prior experience in, 138–40
  reviewing and changing, 135
Membership committee, 134
Membership drive, 69
Mission Research Corporation, 193–94
Morale, 130
  See also Personnel management
Motivation, 116, 117, 130
  See also Personnel management
Mouton, Jane S., 12, 18, 20
Municipal government, relations between fire department and, 50–56

National Fire Academy, 187
National Fire Protection Association, 111, 144, 186–87
Newspapers, 57–60
NFPA No. 1021: Fire Officer Professional Qualifications, 111–13

Obesity, cardiovascular disease and, 142–43
Objectives. *See* Performance-based objectives

Index

Open-door policy, 119–21
Open house, 68–69
Oral examination, fireground officer selection and, 102–7

Paramedic (Advanced Life Support) certification, 187
Participatory management, 30–31
Part paid/part volunteer departments, 83–85
Performance-based objectives, 34
   A-B-C-D method of writing, 173
   training by, 170–73
Performance specifications, 193–96, 201–4
Personality types attracted to volunteer firefighting, 148–51
Personnel files, fireground officer selection and, 100–1
Personnel management, 115–30
   awards, 125–28
   chain of command and, 117–19
   confidentiality of fire department matters, 129–30
   decisions based on a full knowlege of all the facts, 121–22
   feedback and, 122–24
   open-door policy, 119–21
   reprimanding subordinates, 128–29
   showing concern, 125
Physical assessment of applicants, 141–45
Physical condition of applicants, 132

Physical fitness programs, 140–41, 154–55
Physical fitness requirements for firefighters, 144–45
Physical health, 140–41
Physical performance test, predictor-type, 154
Physical requirements and standards, legal aspects of, 153–55
Physician, fire department, 143
Pietrzak, Lawrence M., 194
Planning, 32–47
   action plans, 38–39
   actual process of, 37–43
   apparatus selection and purchase, 191–92
   completion dates, 34–35
   delegating responsibilities, 33–34
   Force Field Analysis method, 44–47
   identifying major project tasks, 33
   outside groups, working with, 35–36
   performance-based objectives and, 34
   prefire, 184–85
   recordkeeping, 36
   a recruitment program, 133–34
   training sessions, 179–80
Police department, 72–74
Politicians, relations with, 50–57
Prefire planning, 53
Probationary period for volunteers, 146–47
Problem solving as teaching method, 179–80
Protection areas, 166–67
Publications, fire service, 61, 158

Public relations, 48–75
  community events and, 53–54, 68–71
  educating the community, 62–66, 71
  fire chiefs association/public safety meetings, 54
  fire service publications and professional events, 61–62
  fund drives and, 51–53
  local government relations, 50–56
  media relations, 57–61
  prefire planning and, 53
  public employees, working with other, 71–75
  state and federal politicians, 56
  training exercises and, 51
Public relations officer, 66–68
Public safety associations, meetings of, 54–55
Purchasing fire apparatus. *See* Apparatus, selecting and purchasing

Radio, 57–58, 61
Rebuilding fire apparatus, 216–17
Reciprocal instruction method, 177–78
Records, 36
Recruitment of members, 131–51
  medical-physical assessment process, 141–45
  membership applications, 133, 135–40
  planning a program for, 133–34
  standards for, 132–33

See also Applicants
Reports, fire incident, 164–66
Reprimanding subordinates, 128–29
Road department, 74

Schleich, Otto A., 194
Schools, fire prevention curriculum in, 35
Selecting fire apparatus. *See* Apparatus, selecting and purchasing
Situational Leadership theory, 22–29
  fire department management and, 27–28
  in realistic terms, 28–29
  task behavior and relationship behavior in, 23–26
Smoke divers program, 158
Smoking, cardiovascular disease and, 142

Task learning method, 177
Television, 57–58, 61
Tests, *See* Oral examination; Written examination
Training, 168–88
  classroom setting for, 173–75
  for emergency driving, 162
  ethnocentric attitudes and, 181
  instructor evaluation, 180–81
  legal issues, 157–59
  at national fire service conferences, 182–83
  by performance-based objectives, 170–73
  planning training sessions, 179–80
  prefire planning and, 184–85

public relations
    considerations, 51
    standards for, 186–87
    state and national programs, 183–84
    teaching methods, 176–79
Tregoe, Benjamin B., 206

Volunteer fire districts, 79–82

Ward, William A., 88
Water and sewage department, 75
Women volunteers, 156
Wright, Howell, 143–44
Written examination, fireground officer selection and, 101–2

Zero-based budgeting (ZBB), 85–96

```
363.378 S
Stewart, Rob.
The volunteer
   firefighters'
management book.
```

Hicksville Public Library
169 Jerusalem Avenue
Hicksville, New York
Telephone Wells 1-1417

Please Do Not Remove
Card From Pocket